2021

Hope you enjoy!
Teri Diamond

TERI DIAMOND

IN TERI'S KITCHEN

Superfoods Simply Made

First edition.

For information contact: Highly Flavored Productions, 1600 Division St., Suite 620, Nashville, TN 37203

Highly Flavored Productions' books may be purchased in bulk for educational, business or sales promotional use.

Layout design and editing by Gretchen C. Mathis

Back cover and recipe photos by Steve Diamond

Cover design and author photos by Thom W. King

Printed by TSE Worldwide Press Inc.

ISBN 1-59975-433-9

SPECIAL THANKS

First and foremost, thanks to God from whom all blessings flow.

Thank you to my husband, Steve, for all of his encouragement and for branching out into the world of photography. Thanks to my son, Cole, for being a willing taste tester. Thanks to my niece, Gretchen Mathis, who did the layout for the cookbook, as well as the editing. Without Gretchen, it would not have been the book that I hoped for. And thanks to my sister, Pam Mathis, whose eye for design added an artistic touch to many of the photos, making them truly special.

We had so much fun creating the settings for the photos. Thanks to Todd Schmidt for his invaluable expertise. Thanks to my brother-in-law, Charles Mathis, for sharing his wonderful marinade. Thanks to my brother, John Dougherty, for believing in me and to my friend, Susan Pomerantz, who is always there for me. Thanks to my mother-in-law, Selma Diamond, who has taught me so much about health and nutrition. Thanks to Kathy Gibson, Henri Handler, Carolyn Dalton, Dawn Nepp, John Vohol, Pam Gaddes and Carol Purser. Thanks to Jean Ann McNally, Connie Bradley, Karen Conrad and Pat Rolfe for all your support. I'll never forget the cooking classes. Thanks to Thom King, Sarah Tse, Vicki Diestelkamp, Flower Mart, David Cook and all my friends at Wild Oats. Thanks to Renee Anzalone for sharing her knowledge of cooking.

For two angels:

*Mama Todd,
who is in Heaven*

&

*my sister,
Pam Mathis,
who is here on
Earth.*

TABLE OF CONTENTS

INTRODUCTION

To me food is a celebration. It's about family and friends coming together to share not only sustenance, but also a connection to each other. My earliest memories of comfort food come from visiting my grandmother, Mama Todd, in her home, as she always prepared feasts with fresh vegetables from her garden. My cousin, Suzanne, and I were often given the task of shelling peas and shucking corn, much to our dismay. I did not have an appreciation for her garden then, but as I harvest my own garden today, I wonder if she is smiling down on me, knowing that she made a difference. It is through her that I carry on the tradition of cooking as a way of expressing love and gratitude for the people who have touched my life.

Food that is good for you really can taste great. I have chosen 11 superfood categories as the focus of this book and have listed both their nutrients and health benefits in the pages that follow. Consistently, they all have anti-cancer properties and aid in the prevention of heart disease. Fortunately, our bodies need a certain amount of fat in order to remain healthy. In fact, using good fats such as those found in olive oil, canola oil, nuts, wild salmon and tuna, help promote optimum health. In some of my dishes, especially those I prepare when we have guests, I even use organic butter and cream. The key is moderation. However, if you are looking for dishes that are low in fat, I suggest you try the *Roasted Red Pepper Soup, Garlic Chicken Stir Fry, Turkey Burgers, Tuna Nicoise, Roasted Carrots in Balsamic Vinegar* and *Romaine Lettuce with Turkey, Strawberries & Hearts of Palm*, among others. Of course, omitting the nuts from certain recipes will also help to reduce the amount of fat. However, nuts are superfoods and are very good for you!

I prepare all of the recipes in this cookbook in my own home, so it is with great pride that I share them with you. I hope you enjoy!

A FEW SUGGESTIONS

Successful cooking is without doubt a process of trial and error. Here, I share with you some helpful hints to keep in mind while cooking. My hope is that you will use them to maximize your time in the kitchen by avoiding some of the pitfalls that I have run into over the years. Cooking is a lot of fun for me and I hope to help create an enjoyable experience for you too!

Before preparing a dish, it is always a good idea to look over the directions. It will give you an idea of how long it will actually take to prepare the dish.

When measuring flour, fill a measuring scoop and sweep a knife across the top edge to level off the flour. This will ensure a more accurate measurement.

When baking, always use the same size pan that is suggested in the recipe for best results.

Use salt sparingly in recipes that call for chicken broth, seasoned bread crumbs, olives or salted butter.

"Part of the fun in cooking is being able to share my creations with others. I love discovering unique or vintage containers and baskets for an added special touch."

Most people are aware that butter is better for you than margarine, but it bears repeating. Margarine contains partially hydrogenated oils, which are harmful to your health. Butter contains no trans fats, which makes it a much healthier choice.

When a recipe calls for mayonnaise, I try to use an organic brand. If an organic mayonnaise is not available, I prefer to use Helmann's.

Don't be afraid to try new things. I have friends who once turned their noses up at the idea of eating *Chicken*

Curry. Those same friends now request that same dish whenever they visit. Obviously, you cannot omit the curry from the *Chicken Curry* or the basil from the *Basil Spread,* but if you prefer shallots to onions or cheddar cheese to jack cheese, simply adjust the recipe to your personal taste. For example, my mother-in-law is lactose intolerant, so I always substitute olive oil for butter and mayonnaise for sour cream or yogurt when preparing a dish for her.

I use organic ingredients when I cook at home. They are more expensive, but worth the extra cost because they contain fewer chemicals. However, this doesn't mean that I only consume organic foods. Restaurants rarely prepare meals with organic ingredients.

I have provided additional ideas for using the sauces and spreads that make up the various dishes in this book. For example, I suggest using the *Basil Spread,* which contains my *Pesto* and is a key ingredient in both the *Bruschetta* and the *Basil Salad Dressing,* as a condiment for the *Salmon Burgers* or as a vegetable dip. I also suggest using my *Tomato Sauce,* a key element in the *Turkey Cannelloni* and the *Pasta in Pink Sauce,*

as sauce for pizza. I have found *Charles' Marinade* to be a fantastic way to spice up both grilled chicken and salmon, as well as other meats. It also adds a smoky flavor to the *Grilled Chicken Salad with Field Greens, Blueberries & Walnuts.* I have even found that the *Roasted Red Pepper Hummus* makes a tasty spread for vegetarian and turkey sandwiches.

Many of the recipes in this book also make great gifts. I like to present my baked goods in a basket lined with a colorful cloth napkin and my sauces, soups and dry goods in decorative jars. Colorful wired ribbon also adds an element of warmth to any container. Experimenting with presentation is a lot of fun and you can find supplies at most art supply stores.

SUPERFOODS

Maintaining good health is directly correlated to the food that we put into our bodies, which is why incorporating the superfoods into our diet is so important. There is a vast amount of literature available online and in the bookstores that discusses the health benefits of the various superfoods. My favorite reference book, one I keep on my kitchen counter at all times, is *Prescription for Nutritional Healing* (Balch & Balch, 2000). I urge you to take a look at this book, as it offers a comprehensive look at the two elements contained in all superfoods that fight cancer in different ways, phytochemicals and antioxidants. Phytochemicals, for example, fight cancer by obstructing the invasion of cells by carcinogens at the most fundamental level. Antioxidants, on the other hand, are specific vitamins, minerals and enzymes that protect cells from the damage that occurs from oxidation. Below, I offer a quick, but complete overview of the 11 superfood categories that I have chosen as the focus of this book.

"Gardening is a gift to your soul and a gift to those you share your harvest with. It teaches us patience, appreciation and gratitude for God's handiwork."

TOMATOES – Tomatoes are rich in lycopene, a powerful antioxidant known to help prevent cancers such as colorectal, prostate, breast, endometrial, lung and pancreatic. They contain vitamins A, B, C, E and K.

BEANS – Beans are a great source of protein, fiber, vitamin B, iron, folate, potassium, magnesium and polyphenols, which are all associated with cancer and heart disease prevention.

SPINACH – Spinach contains manganese, iron, magnesium, beta carotene and vitamins A, B, C, K, E.

It helps prevent cardiovascular disease, cataracts and age-related macular degeneration. Spinach also fights prostate cancer and arthritis.

BLUEBERRIES – Blueberries contain manganese, fiber and vitamins C and E. These superberries are packed with antioxidant phytonutrients called anthocyanidins, which neutralize free radical damage, and help prevent cataracts, glaucoma, varicose veins, peptic ulcers, heart disease and cancer.

SALMON & TUNA – Salmon and Tuna contain LDL, tryptophan, selenium, vitamin B and omega 3 fatty acids, which help boost the good cholesterol. They also have anti-inflammatory effects on joints and lower the risk of stroke, obesity and the body's response to insulin.

TURKEY & CHICKEN BREAST – Turkey and chicken are low-fat sources of protein and contain tryptophan, selenium, niacin, vitamin B and phosphorus. They promote cardiovascular health, aid in regulating blood sugar and lower cancer risk.

NUTS – Nuts contain polyunsaturated fatty acids, protein, fiber, vita-

min E, potassium, folate, magnesium, zinc, selenium, copper, phosphorus, antioxidants and arginine. Nuts promote colon health and reduce the risk of heart disease, diabetes and cancer.

GARLIC – Garlic is rich in sulfur containing compounds, including thiosulfinates, sulfoxides and dithiins, as well as flavonoids, such as quercetin. Garlic is known for it's anti-cancer properties as well as it's cardiovascular benefits. It also has anti-inflammatory, anti-bacterial and anti-viral properties.

RED & ORANGE VEGETABLES – Red and orange vegetables contain molybdenum, manganese, folate, carotenoids and vitamins A, B, C, E, and K. They help prevent heart disease, osteoarthritis and rheumatoid arthritis, as well as colon cancer, prostate cancer and cancers of the cervix, bladder and pancreas.

BROCCOLI & CRUCIFEROUS VEGETABLES – Broccoli and cruciferous vegetables contain calcium, magnesium, iron, folate, zinc, fiber, phytochemicals and vitamins A, B and C. They help prevent heart disease, breast cancer and birth defects. They also help strengthen bones, boost the immune system and protect against ulcers and rheumatoid arthritis.

OATS – Oats contain manganese, selenium, phosphorus, vitamin B1, magnesium and fiber. They lower cholesterol and blood pressure, reduce the risk of cardiovascular disease and enhance immune response to bacterial infections. Oats also contain cancer fighting properties and help stabilize blood sugar.

GUIDE

✶ ✶ ✶ ✶ ✶ ✶

The above icon denotes how many superfoods are used in each recipe. In addition to the 11 superfood categories that I have included in this book, there are many other healthy ingredients that also promote good health, such as asparagas, artichoke hearts, romaine lettuce, red leaf lettuce, shallots, strawberries, currants and olives.

STARTERS

If you are serving a starter, it will be the first thing your guests will taste, so it is important to choose something that compliments the meal and also your guests' palate. For example, the *Bruschetta* goes well with any of the pasta dishes. The *Black Bean & Corn Salsa* is a perfect starter for the *Grilled Salmon, Grilled Chicken, Tuna Steak, Salmon Burgers* and *Turkey Burgers*. More than likely, you already know what your close friends and family prefer to eat. If you are serving someone new, it is appropriate to give them a choice before preparing the dish.

Some of my favorite starters, such as the *Tomato Artichoke Soup, Mushrooms Stuffed with Turkey Sausage* and *Roasted Red Pepper Soup* can be served with a salad and bread to become a complete meal. The *Bruschetta, Basil Spread, Baked Garlic & Goat Cheese, Spinach & Artichoke Dip, Roasted Red Pepper Hummus, Toasted Walnuts with Rosemary* and *Black Bean & Corn Salsa* are great choices for entertaining a large group of guests. This section also provides many vegetarian choices. Ultimately, you are sure to find the perfect starter to compliment any meal and accommodate any taste.

The superfoods featured in this section include: garlic, tomatoes, red peppers, carrots, garbanzo beans, black beans, spinach, walnuts, pine nuts and turkey.

Tomato Artichoke Soup

Roasted Red Pepper Hummus

Basil Spread

Mushrooms Stuffed with Turkey Sausage

Black Bean & Corn Salsa

Bruschetta

Spinach & Artichoke Dip

Baked Garlic & Goat Cheese on Baguette Rounds

Toasted Walnuts with Rosemary

Roasted Red Pepper Soup

TOMATO ARTICHOKE SOUP

I love this hearty soup. The creamy blue cheese enhances the tangy flavor of the tomatoes and artichokes. For lunch, I serve it as a complete meal with sourdough bread, iced tea and my *Oatmeal Almond Cookies*.

1 28 ounce can chopped plum tomatoes

1 28 ounce can organic crushed tomatoes with basil

1 medium onion, chopped

3 cloves garlic, minced

2 14 ounce cans quartered artichokes

3 cups chicken broth

⅓ cup reduced fat cream cheese

4 ounces blue cheese crumbles

2 tablespoons olive oil

2 tablespoons butter

Salt and pepper to taste

1. In a large pot, sauté onions in olive oil and butter. When onions become soft, add garlic and sauté for an additional minute.

2. Add tomatoes, artichokes, chicken stock, salt and pepper to the onions and garlic. Bring to a boil and simmer for 20 minutes.

3. Add reduced fat cream cheese and blue cheese crumbles. Combine thoroughly and simmer for an additional 10 minutes.

4. Remove from heat and serve.

ROASTED RED PEPPER HUMMUS

This is such a healthy appetizer and is especially tasty when paired with fresh pita bread. Plus, if you serve it in a hollowed-out red pepper, accompanied by Kalamata olives, cherry tomatoes, cucumber and carrot sticks, you will be consuming five super foods!

1 15 ounce can garbanzo beans, drained (reserve ¼ cup of liquid)

2 large cloves garlic, pressed

Juice of 1 large lemon

¾ cup tahini paste

¾ cup roasted red bell pepper

¼ teaspoon salt

¼ teaspoon pepper

1. Process red pepper in a food processor until a paste forms.

2. Add garbanzo beans, garlic, lemon, tahini paste, salt and pepper. Process until smooth.

3. Add ¼ cup of liquid reserved from the garbanzo beans and process once again.

4. Taste and adjust seasonings. You may prefer to add additional lemon, salt or pepper.

Note: A great way to consume any leftover *Red Pepper Hummus* is to combine it with a bit of mayonnaise and use it as a spread for sandwiches.

BASIL SPREAD

✳ ✳

The arrival of summer is always a delight for gastronomic aficionados, as it yields a myriad of aromatic and flavorful herbs that stir the senses and awaken the soul. I especially enjoy using freshly cut basil from my garden for both its savory sweet flavor and its versatility in cooking. I use this *Basil Spread*, which I consider to be a staple in my kitchen, on everything from my *Bruschetta* to turkey sandwiches with tomato and baby spinach. It also makes a delicious dip for vegetables and is wonderful served on crackers.

2 cups fresh basil leaves

4 tablespoons pine nuts

½ cup freshly grated parmesan

½ cup olive oil

2 large cloves of garlic, pressed

Salt to taste

1 cup of mayonnaise

1. Place pine nuts in a food processor and process until completely ground.

2. Add the basil, parmesan cheese, garlic, olive oil and salt to the ground pine nuts and process until a smooth paste forms.

3. Add 1 heaping tablespoon of basil mixture to the mayonnaise and blend well to form the spread. Add additional basil mixture to create a stronger flavor, if you prefer.

Note: Place remainder of basil paste in an air tight container and cover with a thin layer of olive oil. The sealed container will last for approximately one week in the refrigerator or can be frozen for later use. You can also use the basil paste to make *Basil Salad Dressing* (pg. 59).

MUSHROOMS STUFFED WITH TURKEY SAUSAGE

My *Mushrooms Stuffed with Turkey Sausage* make a great appetizer, but I also like to serve them as an entrée, accompanied by my *Garden Vegetable Salad* and freshly baked bread.

24 large mushrooms

1 pound ground turkey sausage

1 tablespoon water, if needed

1 large shallot, minced

Ground pepper to taste

2 tablespoons light olive oil

½ cup seasoned bread crumbs

1 large clove garlic, pressed

6 tablespoons butter, plus 3 tablespoons for brushing caps

1 cup grated jack cheese

1. Preheat oven to 350 degrees.

2. Remove the stems from the mushrooms, wash caps and brush with 3 tablespoons of melted butter. Place in a baking dish.

3. Sauté shallot in olive oil until soft, then add turkey sausage. Once sausage is cooked, drain excess liquid and return to burner.

4. Add garlic and ground pepper and cook for 1 minute.

5. Add bread crumbs and the remaining 6 tablespoons of melted butter. If stuffing seems dry, add a tablespoon of water.

6. Remove from heat and spoon mixture into the mushroom caps. Dribble a few drops of melted butter onto each stuffed mushroom and top with jack cheese.

7. Bake for 15 minutes or until the mushrooms are fully cooked and the cheese has melted.

Note: As a garnish, I like to use steamed snap peas.

BLACK BEAN & CORN SALSA

✳ ✳ ✳

There are many variations of this healthy salsa. While some utilize lime juice or Italian dressing, I prefer to use a well aged balsamic vinegar, as it perfectly complements the red pepper and avocado and adds a certain zest that the others lack. Although traditionally served with tortilla chips, I also love to use my version of this salsa as a flavorful relish atop grilled salmon or chicken.

1 15 ounce can black beans, drained

1 small can sweet yellow corn

½ cup green bell pepper, diced

½ cup red bell pepper, diced

1 tablespoon fresh cilantro, finely chopped

1 avocado, cubed

1 tomato, diced

⅔ cup olive oil

⅓ cup balsamic vinegar

1 large shallot, minced

Salt and pepper

1. In a large bowl, combine black beans, corn, green pepper, red pepper and cilantro.

2. Season with salt and pepper and lightly stir.

3. Add avocado and tomato.

4. In a bowl, slowly whisk olive oil into balsamic vinegar. Add shallots and pour into black bean mixture.

5. Stir until combined. Serve with tortilla chips.

BRUSCHETTA

✳ ✳ ✳

In Italy, bruschetta al pomodoro is typically served as an appetizer in which plump Mediterranean tomatoes are chopped, tossed with salt and olive oil and served atop a slice of grilled, dense Italian bread that has been rubbed generously with a raw clove of garlic. In my version of this simple, vitamin packed dish, I add balsamic vinegar to the tomato mixture and use my *Basil Spread* in lieu of the garlic to create a creamier, more substantial prelude to any meal. While it is wonderful served before my *Pasta in Pink Sauce* or *Linguine with Pomodoro Sauce*, I have found that it also makes a delicious light lunch when served on its own.

French baguette or sour dough bread

8 ounces fresh whole milk mozzarella, sliced

1 container cherry tomatoes, halved

¼ cup olive oil

Balsamic vinegar to taste

Salt and pepper to taste

Basil Spread (pg. 22)

1. Slice French bread into ½ inch rounds. Place on baking sheet and toast in oven.

2. Place cherry tomatoes in a large bowl. Add salt, pepper, olive oil and desired amount of balsamic vinegar. Mix well and set aside.

3. Cover each slice of toasted bread with *Basil Spread* and place a slice of mozzarella on top.

4. Top with tomato mixture and serve immediately.

Option: If you don't have any *Basil Spread* on hand, try it the Italian way and gently rub a peeled clove of garlic over the toasted bread before adding the mozzarella and tomato mixture. Top with chopped fresh basil before serving.

SPINACH & ARTICHOKE DIP

✳ ✳ ✳

This is one of my very favorite appetizers to prepare for guests. Not only does it look great served in the fresh bread bowl, but the intense flavors of horseradish and garlic make this dish absolutely delicious!

1 6 ounce bag fresh spinach

¾ cup artichokes, chopped

1 8 ounce container cream cheese

1 cup mayonnaise

1 cup parmesan cheese, shredded

1 tablespoon pure horse-radish

8 sun dried tomatoes (optional)

1 clove garlic, pressed

Juice of ¼ lemon

Salt and pepper to taste

1 loaf of sour dough or Tuscan bread

1. Rinse spinach and place directly in a large heated pan without drying. Season with salt and pepper, cover pan and cook over medium heat for 2 minutes.

2. Thoroughly drain liquid from the pan. Remove spinach, chop and drain once more with a paper towel.

3. Place spinach in a medium size bowl and add lemon juice and garlic. Mix well.

4. Stir 1 tablespoon of pure horseradish into the spinach mixture. Set aside.

5. In a large bowl, use a hand mixer to blend the cream cheese and parmesan cheese until smooth. Add mayonnaise.

6. Boil sun dried tomatoes for 2 minutes or until soft. Chop into small pieces.

7. With a large spoon, combine the spinach mixture with the cheese mixture.

8. Add the artichokes and sun dried tomatoes and stir lightly until blended.

9. Hollow out a round loaf of sour dough or Tuscan bread and spoon dip into loaf. Use leftover bread for dipping.

Note: The dip can also be served on top of Belgian endive as an hors d'oeuvre or with crackers and carrot sticks.

BAKED GARLIC & GOAT CHEESE ON BAGUETTE ROUNDS

This fabulous, Mediterranean inspired appetizer boasts a host of healthy ingredients, such as olive oil, garlic, Greek Kalamata olives and sun dried tomatoes from Italy. Paired with a French baguette and mild goat cheese, the smoky taste of baked garlic makes these incredible crostini the perfect hors d'oeuvre for get-togethers.

1 large garlic head

8 sun dried tomatoes

Olive oil

Mild goat cheese, such as Chavrie

Kalamata olives, pitted and diced

Baguette, sliced

Asparagus tips

1. Preheat oven to 350 degrees.

2. Do not peel garlic. Cut the top off of the bulb with a sharp knife. Drizzle with olive oil and bake for 20 minutes in a covered garlic roaster. Then, remove the cover and bake for an additional 15 minutes. If you do not have a garlic roaster, wrap the garlic bulb in aluminum foil, place it on a baking sheet and bake according to above directions.

3. Once roasted, remove from oven and allow to cool.

4. Toast baguette rounds under a broiler.

5. Boil sun dried tomatoes for 1 to 2 minutes or until soft, then cut into small strips.

6. Steam asparagus tips for 1 to 2 minutes and set aside.

7. Squeeze baked garlic pods out of bulb into a small bowl and mash with a fork to form a paste.

8. Spread a layer of roasted garlic on each baguette round, followed by a layer of goat cheese.

9. Wrap a sun dried tomato strip around an asparagus tip and place in middle of baguette slice. Sprinkle olive pieces around the asparagus and serve.

Note: Strips of prosciutto can be substituted for the sun dried tomatoes if you prefer.

TOASTED WALNUTS WITH ROSEMARY

I always keep these delicious nuts on hand and serve them with cheese, crackers and red grapes when I have unexpected guests. They also make a wonderful gift for family and friends.

4 cups walnuts

2 tablespoons olive oil

2 teaspoons fresh rosemary, minced

½ teaspoon salt

1. Preheat oven to 250 degrees.

2. Place walnuts in a bowl, add olive oil and salt. Stir until walnuts are well-coated.

3. Pour walnuts onto a large baking sheet and bake for 35 minutes, stirring half way through.

4. Remove walnuts from oven and pour into a large container.

5. Sprinkle with rosemary and mix well.

6. Allow the walnuts to cool thoroughly and store in air tight container.

ROASTED RED PEPPER SOUP

When I have guests and serve this savory soup as a starter, I like to add ½ cup of cream to give it a richer, more decadent flavor. This recipe yields approximately 4 appetizer sized portions, which are best served in cups. If you prefer to serve it in bowls, simply double the recipe.

3 red bell peppers

3 shallots, minced

1 cup chicken broth

½ teaspoon herbes de provence

2 tablespoons olive oil

Salt to taste

1. Cut peppers in half and remove the core and seeds.

2. Place the peppers, cut side down, on a baking tin or roasting pan. Broil for 5 minutes or until the peppers become charred.

3. Remove peppers from oven, seal tightly in paper bag and set aside for 10 minutes. This technique will cause the peppers to sweat, allowing you to easily peel away the charred skin.

4. After 10 minutes, remove the peppers from the paper bag and peel and cut into 3 inch pieces.

5. Sauté shallots in olive oil on medium to low heat until translucent.

6. Add the roasted red peppers, herbes de provence and salt to the skillet and continue to sauté for 5 minutes. Remove from heat.

7. Puree a large spoonful of the shallot and red pepper mixture in a food processor.

8. Add 2 tablespoons of the chicken broth and process once again.

9. Pour mixture into medium size pot and repeat steps 7 and 8 until all of the red pepper mixture has been used. Add any remaining broth to the soup. Heat and serve.

SALADS

My husband and I love salads and often prepare them as an entire meal. In fact, with the exception of the *Garden Vegetable Salad*, the *Caesarless Salad* and the *Spinach Salad with Baked Goat Cheese*, all of the recipes in this section are substantial enough to substitute for a heavier dish and satisfy any appetite. And if you happen to crave one of the three lighter salads, simply add grilled chicken, salmon or tuna and it can be served as a main dish as well.

In this section, I have also included five salad dressings for you to enjoy: *Vinaigrette, Basil Salad Dressing, Balsamic Vinaigrette, Creamy Vinaigrette* and *Louie Dressing.* Many of these dressings call for olive oil, so it is worth noting that there is a wide variety of olive oil available on the market, ranging from light to deep and fruity in flavor. It is all a matter of taste, so it is a good idea to try a few in order to find the one that best suits your palate. I would suggest you do the same for balsamic vinegar. While all balsamic vinegars are made from the Trebbiano grape, their flavors differ greatly by crop and length of fermentation. Personally, I prefer a slightly sweet balsamic, like Lucini Gran Riserva Balsamico (aged ten years), to those that are more acidic. As you explore, I am sure that you will find one to satisfy your taste.

The superfoods featured in this section include: salmon, tuna, chicken, turkey, tomatoes, red peppers, spinach, almonds, walnuts, blueberries, garlic and watercress.

TUNA SALAD WITH CURRANTS IN TOMATO

I love serving my version of this traditional salad for lunch. Not only does it look great stuffed in a tomato surrounded by baby red leaf lettuce, but the currants perfectly complement the other ingredients by adding just a hint of sweetness.

1 bag baby red leaf lettuce

2 to 4 large tomatoes

1 large can albacore white tuna, packed in spring water

1 stalk celery, diced

2 boiled eggs, diced

½ cup currants

½ cup mayonnaise

Freshly ground pepper

Vinaigrette (pg. 61)

1. Drain water from tuna and place in a medium size bowl. With a fork, mash the tuna until there are no chunks.

2. Mix together celery, boiled eggs, currants and the desired amount of pepper. Add mayonnaise and mix well. Set aside.

3. Fill each plate with a handful of lettuce and place a tomato face down on top of each pile.

4. With a sharp knife, make two slices downward through the tomato in the shape of an x, leaving about ½ inch at the bottom uncut. Make a third slice through the middle of the x and spread the tomato open.

5. Spoon tuna salad into the tomato, drizzle *Vinaigrette* on lettuce and serve.

GARDEN VEGETABLE SALAD

I generally serve this simple, garden fresh salad with *Turkey Chili* or one of my pasta dishes, such as the *Pasta in Pink Sauce* or the *Bowtie Pasta with Pesto*. It is easy to prepare and compliments those dishes very well.

1 bag organic mixed greens

2 cups sliced mushrooms

1 cucumber, peeled and sliced

1 red pepper, cut into strips

1 avocado, sliced

12 cherry tomatoes, halved

Seasoned croutons

1. Combine all ingredients in a large salad bowl.

2. Add any salad dressing of your choice.

3. Toss and serve.

TUNA NICOISE

✤ ✤ ✤

In my version of this popular, low fat salad, I have chosen to omit the boiled potatoes that are traditionally included. I don't feel that they add enough flavor to justify the extra carbohydrates. However, you may choose to add them.

½ bag mixed greens

French green beans

1 large can white tuna

Fresh white button mushrooms, sliced

Tomatoes, sliced

8 nicoise olives

Vinaigrette (pg. 61)

1. Steam green beans for 2 to 3 minutes and set aside.

2. Divide the mixed greens between two plates and top each with half of the tuna.

3. Top the mixed greens with green beans, olives, sliced mushrooms and tomatoes.

4. Drizzle *Vinaigrette* over salad and serve. Serves 2.

Note: If serving more than two people, simply use an entire bag of greens and serve on a platter, as shown above.

POACHED SALMON SALAD

� ✰ ✰ ✰

This delicious salad features one of my favorite food and herb combinations, salmon with basil. The *Basil Salad Dressing* perfectly compliments the flavor of the salmon, creating a light and healthy meal.

½ pound poached salmon

1 bag organic mixed greens

1 bunch asparagus tips

1 cucumber, sliced

Tomatoes, sliced

1 avocado, sliced

Croutons

Lemon

Basil Salad Dressing (pg. 59)

1. Steam asparagus for 2 minutes and set aside.

2. Squeeze lemon over salmon, place in parchment paper and twist the ends to close. Poach salmon in a pan of boiling water for 10 minutes.

3. Remove from heat and allow the salmon to cool.

4. Prepare salad with the remaining ingredients and place pieces of poached salmon on top.

5. Drizzle with *Basil Salad Dressing* and serve.

CAESARLESS SALAD

Caesar Salad is one of the classic accompaniments to an array of entrees, from fish and poultry to pasta. The original version of this particular recipe for Caesar Salad was created by my brother, Randy, who had an amazing flair for cooking. For the purposes of this book, I have chosen to omit the two raw egg yolks from the dressing—thus the name, *Caesarless Salad*.

4 flat anchovy filets

4 cloves garlic, pressed

5 tablespoons Worcestershire Sauce

½ teaspoon dry mustard

1 teaspoon country style Dijon mustard

4 dashes Tabasco Sauce

Juice of 1 lemon

1 tablespoon apple cider vinegar

½ teaspoon seasoned pepper

¾ to 1 cup olive oil

1 cup shredded parmesan cheese

1 head romaine lettuce

1 box seasoned croutons

1. Close eyes (optional) and mash anchovies in a small bowl until a paste is formed.

2. Add garlic, Worcestershire Sauce, dry mustard, country style mustard, seasoned pepper, Tabasco Sauce, lemon juice and apple cider vinegar. Slowly whisk in olive oil.

3. Transfer entire dressing mixture to a large salad bowl.

4. Tear lettuce into 3 inch pieces and place in the bowl containing the salad dressing. Toss once.

5. Add croutons and parmesan cheese. Toss again and serve.

GRILLED CHICKEN SALAD WITH FIELD GREENS BLUEBERRIES & WALNUTS

Although this salad is delicious prepared with simple grilled chicken, I especially enjoy it when I have leftover *Grilled Chicken with Charles' Marinade*. It really spices it up!

2 boneless chicken breasts, grilled and cut into strips

1 bag organic field greens

1 cup blueberries

1 cup walnuts

Blue cheese crumbles

8 cherry tomatoes, halved

Creamy Vinaigrette (pg. 60)

1. Place a handful of organic field greens on each of the plates.

2. Divide the blueberries, walnuts and tomatoes equally among the plates.

3. Top with chicken strips and sprinkle with blue cheese crumbles.

4. Drizzle *Creamy Vinaigrette* on each salad and serve. Serves 4.

CURRIED CHICKEN SALAD ON WATERCRESS

✳ ✳ ✳ ✳

I like to serve my *Curried Chicken Salad* on watercress. Not only is watercress a cruciferous vegetable that is high in fiber, vitamin C and phytonutrients, but it also helps to prevent cancer. If you prefer, you may also use mixed greens with this salad. However, I find the peppery flavor of watercress to be a perfect match for the exotic taste of curry.

1 pound boneless chicken breasts

½ cup red pepper, diced

⅓ cup celery, diced

¾ cup red seedless grapes, sliced

¼ cup oven roasted almonds, sliced

2 bunches watercress

1 can hearts of palm, sliced

strawberries

1 tablespoon mild curry paste

¾ cup sour cream

½ cup of mayonnaise

2 tablespoons honey

1. Boil chicken breasts with a dash of salt for 15 minutes in a medium size pan.

2. Drain hot water from the pan and add cold water in order to cool the chicken. Set aside.

3. In a small bowl, mix together the sour cream, mayonnaise, curry paste and honey. Set aside. This mix can be adjusted to suit your taste. If you prefer a stronger taste of curry, add an additional teaspoon. If you prefer a sweeter taste, add an additional teaspoon of honey.

4. Cut chicken into small pieces, place in a large bowl.

5. Add red pepper, celery, grapes and almonds.

6. Fold in curry mixture and mix well.

7. Place a handful of watercress on each plate and spoon a large mound of the chicken salad mixture onto the watercress.

8. Surround with sliced strawberries and sliced hearts of palm.

SHRIMP SALAD ON SPINACH WITH LOUIE DRESSING

This vitamin packed salad that features a myriad of healthy foods is another one of my favorites. It is healthy and tastes great. Who could ask for more?

1 10 ounce bag baby spinach

1 cucumber, sliced

12 cherry tomatoes, halved

2 boiled eggs, sliced

1 avocado, sliced

1 pound boiled shrimp

Louie Dressing (pg. 59)

1. Place a handful of spinach on each plate.

2. Arrange remaining ingredients on top of the spinach. I like to line the egg slices up on one side of the plate and the avocado on the opposite side, with the shrimp in the center. I intersperse the cucumbers and tomatoes throughout the dish.

3. Spoon a generous portion of *Louie Dressing* over salad and serve. Serves 4.

ROMAINE LETTUCE WITH TURKEY, STRAWBERRIES & HEARTS OF PALM

This quick, but satisfying salad was my inspiration for creating the *Creamy Vinaigrette*. It goes especially well with fresh rosemary bread or foccacia.

1 bag hearts of romaine

5 slices honey smoked turkey, cut into strips

12 strawberries, halved

1 small can hearts of palm, sliced

1 small container goat cheese crumbles

1 cup mushrooms, sliced

1 cup seasoned croutons

Creamy Vinaigrette (pg. 60)

1. Place a handful of romaine lettuce on each plate.

2. Top lettuce with turkey, strawberries, mushrooms and hearts of palm.

3. Sprinkle each salad with goat cheese crumbles and croutons.

4. Drizzle *Creamy Vinaigrette* over salads and serve.

Serves 4.

SPINACH SALAD WITH BAKED GOAT CHEESE

✳ ✳ ✳

This is one of my all-time favorite salads. The warm, pecan encrusted goat cheese tastes incredible when paired with the *Balsamic Vinaigrette*. This is an impressive, yet easy, salad to serve when entertaining guests.

1 5 ounce bag baby spinach

1 8 ounce log goat cheese

16 sweet grape tomatoes, halved

16 mushrooms, sliced

½ cup ground pecans

Freshly ground pepper

8 baguette slices

Balsamic Vinaigrette (pg. 60)

1. Place spinach, cherry tomatoes and mushrooms in a large bowl and season with freshly ground pepper. Set aside.

2. Slice goat cheese into eight equal pieces and coat one side of each piece with the ground pecans. Set aside.

3. Place baguette slices on a baking sheet and toast them under the broiler until lightly browned.

4. Remove the baguette slices from under the broiler, flip each one over to expose the untoasted side and place a slice of goat cheese (pecan side up) on each one. Place under broiler for 3 minutes or until cheese is soft.

5. Toss salad with *Balsamic Vinaigrette* and divide equally between 4 plates. Top each salad with 2 goat cheese rounds and serve.

BASIL SALAD DRESSING

This is another one of those versatile recipes that I utilize in many different ways. I especially enjoy it served atop my *Poached Salmon Salad*, but I've also used it as a dip for vegetables.

3 tablespoons basil paste
(pg. 22)

¾ cup sour cream

¼ cup mayonnaise

¼ cup milk

1. Combine all ingredients in a medium size bowl and mix well.

2. Serve over your choice of salad.

LOUIE DRESSING

My creamy, rich version of the classic Louie Dressing is a wonderful match for my *Shrimp Salad on Spinach*, but it also goes well with a traditional cobb salad.

½ cup mayonnaise

¼ cup heavy cream

2 tablespoon chives

2 tablespoons celery, minced

3 tablespoons chili sauce

2 teaspoons lemon juice

½ teaspoon horseradish

Ground pepper to taste

1. Combine mayonnaise and heavy cream in a small bowl.

2. Add chili sauce, horseradish, chives and celery. Mix well.

3. Add lemon juice and ground pepper. Blend well.

4. Serve over the *Shrimp Salad on Spinach* or any other salad.

CREAMY VINAIGRETTE

This dressing perfectly complements the *Romaine Lettuce with Turkey, Strawberries & Hearts of Palm* and the *Grilled Chicken Salad with Field Greens, Blueberries & Walnuts.*

2 tablespoons lemon juice

¼ cup rice wine vinegar

2 tablespoons Dijon mustard

1 large clove garlic, pressed

2 medium shallots, pressed

1 ½ cups canola oil

1 teaspoon sugar

¼ cup chopped fresh basil

Salt and pepper to taste

1. In a bowl, whisk together vinegar, lemon juice, mustard, garlic and shallots.

2. Slowly whisk in the canola oil until well blended.

3. Add suger. Taste and add more sugar if too tart.

4. Season with salt and pepper and add the chopped basil. Mix well.

BALSAMIC VINAIGRETTE

This dressing is perfect for the *Spinach Salad with Baked Goat Cheese.* I also use it for my *Black Bean & Corn Salsa* and, on occasion, for my *Garden Vegetable Salad.*

⅔ cup balsamic vinegar

1 ⅓ cup olive oil

2 large shallots

Salt and ground pepper

1. In a medium size bowl, slowly whisk olive oil into the balsamic vinegar. If using a tart balsamic vinegar, add 1 teaspoon of sugar.

2. Once blended, add salt and freshly ground pepper.

3. Put shallots through a garlic press and blend into dressing.

4. Store in a tightly sealed container

VINAIGRETTE

My *Vinaigrette* is a versatile condiment that works well with salads, such as the *Tuna Salad with Currants in Tomato* and the *Tuna Nicoise*, and with side dishes like the *Wild Rice Salad*.

4 tablespoons Dijon mustard

6 tablespoons rice wine vinegar

1 cup olive oil

2 shallots, minced

1 teaspoon sugar

Salt and pepper to taste

1. Whisk together the Dijon mustard and rice wine vinegar.

2. Slowly add olive oil a little at a time while whisking to emulsify.

3. Add sugar and blend further.

4. Once blended, add shallots to the mixture and a touch of salt and pepper.

ENTRÉES

When my son was born, I became a vegetarian for eight months and my endless pursuit of the perfect meatless entrée began. During that time, I began to experiment more with pasta and created such recipes as my *Pasta in Pink Sauce with Sun Dried Tomatoes & Artichokes* and my *Bowtie Pasta with Pesto*. I have since added fish, chicken and turkey to my diet, but I often look forward to a light, yet satisfying, vegetarian dish. In this section, I offer a host of tantalizing recipes for both those who choose not to eat animal protein, as well as those who do.

During the week, I prepare more of the simple dishes for my family. We especially enjoy the *Turkey Stuffed Peppers,* the *Linguine with Pomodoro Sauce,* the *Turkey Burgers,* and the *Garlic Chicken Stir Fry.* For guests and special occasions, I serve the more elaborate dishes like the *Turkey Cannelloni, Chicken Curry with Basmati Rice* and the *Pasta in Pink Sauce with Sun Dried Tomatoes & Artichokes.* Whatever your dietary restrictions, I hope that some of these entrées will become your family's favorites too.

The superfoods featured in this section include: turkey, chicken, red peppers, yellow peppers, orange peppers, tomatoes, garlic, broccoli, tuna, salmon, oats, pistachios and cashews.

TURKEY CANNELLONI

My *Turkey Cannelloni* is the very first dish that I created on my own. In fact, I have served more *Turkey Cannelloni* for my relatives than any other dish. This entrée features both homemade béchamel and tomato sauce. These two sauces balance each other out perfectly, as the white béchamel neutralizes the natural acidity of the red tomatoes. If you'd like to add an additional superfood, a cup of chopped fresh spinach works really well when added to the filling.

Filling:

1 pound ground turkey

1 small onion, chopped

2 large cloves garlic, pressed

¾ teaspoon dried oregano

¼ cup parmesan cheese, grated

8 sun dried tomatoes, diced

2 cups Tomato Sauce (pg. 65)

1 cup button mushrooms, chopped

2 tablespoons olive oil

12 cannelloni or manicotti shells

Freshly ground pepper

3 tablespoons parmesan cheese for topping

3 tablespoons butter for topping

1. Preheat oven to 375 degrees.

2. For the tomato sauce, sauté onion and garlic in a large pan until the onion is soft.

3. Add tomatoes, tomato paste, sugar, salt and ground pepper. You can also add ½ teaspoon of oregano, if you prefer. Cook for 25 minutes over medium heat or until mixture thickens.

4. Remove tomato sauce from heat, add parmesan cheese and process the mixture in a food processor until a smooth sauce forms. Set aside.

5. For the filling, heat olive oil in a large pan and sauté the onions until soft. Add mushrooms and garlic and sauté for an additional 2 minutes. Add turkey, ground pepper and oregano to the pan and cook until done.

6. While turkey is cooking, boil water in a small pan, add sun dried tomatoes and cook for 2 minutes or until soft. Remove tomatoes, cut into small pieces and set aside.

7. Add parmesan cheese, sun dried tomatoes and 2 cups of the tomato sauce to the turkey mixture. The remaining tomato sauce will be used to top the cannelloni prior to baking.

Tomato Sauce:

1 28 ounce can diced plum tomatoes

1 small onion, chopped

2 large cloves garlic, minced

1 small can tomato paste

1 teaspoon sugar

⅓ cup parmesan cheese

4 tablespoons olive oil

Salt and pepper to taste

Béchamel Sauce:

1 stick butter

1 cup cream

1 cup milk

½ cup flour

Salt and white pepper

8. Boil 6 quarts of water and a drop of olive oil in a large pot. Cook manicotti shells for 9 minutes or until done. Drain the hot water from the pot and add cold water. When the pasta has cooled, remove from water.

9. Spread a layer of tomato sauce across the bottom of a baking dish. Stuff each manicotti shell with the turkey mixture and lay the cannelloni side by side in the dish.

10. For the béchamel, heat butter in a medium size sauce pan. When the butter melts, remove from heat, add the flour and blend with a whisk. Return to heat and gradually add milk and cream, while continuing to whisk. When the sauce comes to a boil, reduce heat and stir for a few additional minutes until the sauce thickens. Remove from heat and season with salt and pepper.

11. Pour the white sauce over the cannelloni. With a spoon, pour a line of tomato sauce over each cannelloni. Sprinkle with parmesan cheese and dot with butter.

12. Bake for 20 minutes.

CHICKEN CURRY WITH BASMATI RICE

✳ ✳ ✳

My husband, Steve, absolutely loves this dish. I usually prepare it when we have company for dinner, not only because it offers a beautiful presentation and exotic flavor, but also because it works well with various wines, particularly with Conundrum. If you prefer a red wine, GSM works well.

4 boneless chicken breasts

2 cloves garlic

1 medium onion, chopped

1 cup sliced mushrooms

½ cup pistachios

1 cup plain yogurt

1 cup sour cream

2 tablespoons mild curry paste

2 tablespoons honey

2 tablespoons light olive oil

1 ½ cups basmati rice

1. Place chicken in a pan and cover with water. Bring water to a boil and cook for 12 minutes. Remove, allow to cool and cut into bite size pieces. Set aside.

2. Combine yogurt, sour cream, curry paste and honey in a small bowl. Set aside. If you are unable to find curry paste, substitute 1 teaspoon cumin, 1 teaspoon coriander and 1 small tin of curry powder.

3. Saute onion in olive oil until soft. Add mushrooms and garlic.

4. Once the mushrooms are cooked, add chicken and the curry mixture.

5. Remove from heat, add the pistachios and mix well. Transfer to a serving dish.

6. Rinse the basmati rice.

7. Bring 3½ cups of water to a boil, add rice and stir once. When rice begins to boil again, lower the heat, cover and simmer for 15 minutes or until the water has been absorbed.

8. Once cooked, remove rice from heat and allow to stand for 5 minutes. Stir and transfer to a serving dish.

TURKEY STUFFED RED, YELLOW & ORANGE PEPPERS

This is a dish that I make often in my home and usually serve with mashed potatoes, steamed broccoli and homemade corn muffins. These *Stuffed Peppers* make great leftovers and taste just as good the next day when they are reheated in the microwave oven.

6 peppers (red, yellow, orange)

1 small onion, chopped

½ cup butter, melted

1 large clove garlic, pressed

1 pound ground turkey

1½ cups seasoned bread crumbs

2½ cups chicken broth

1 tablespoon olive oil

Ground pepper to taste

Butter for topping

1. Preheat oven to 350 degrees.

2. Cut the tops off of the peppers, deseed and parboil them in a large pan of water for 10 minutes with tops. Remove and place on baking dish.

3. Sauté onions in olive oil until they become soft. Add ground turkey and cook over medium heat until done.

4. Add garlic and pepper.

5. Add a fourth of the bread crumbs along with enough broth to moisten them. Gradually add the remaining bread crumbs and broth, a little at a time.

6. After adding the last of the bread crumbs, add the melted butter (instead of the broth) and mix well. If the turkey mixture seems dry, add a little more broth (you will have approximately 1 cup of broth left over).

7. Fill each of the peppers to the top with the turkey mixture, top with a dot of butter and cover with pepper tops. Add remainder of broth to baking dish.

8. Bake for 25 minutes and serve.

GRILLED SALMON WITH CHARLES' MARINADE

My brother-in-law, Charles, created this sauce decades ago to marinate steaks. It is absolutely delicious! In our home, we use it to marinate salmon and chicken.

4 salmon fillets

½ cup Worcestershire Sauce

2 tablespoons Colgin's Liquid Smoke

2 tablespoons Lawry's Lemon Pepper Seasoning

1 stick butter

1 onion (or more), sliced

Juice of ½ lemon

Coarse ground pepper

1. Heat Worcestershire Sauce, liquid smoke, lemon pepper and butter in a medium size pan.

2. When butter is melted, add onion slices, lemon juice and ground pepper. Bring to a boil, then reduce heat and simmer for an additional 15 minutes.

3. Wash salmon and place in a deep dish or pan. Pour sauce, including the onions, over salmon and marinade for 30 minutes to an hour.

4. Grill salmon over an open flame for 5 to 6 minutes on each side (depending on thickness), while continuously basting.

5. Place sautéed onions in a wire basket or aluminum foil and cook on the grill with the salmon.

6. Top salmon with onions and serve immediately.

LINGUINE WITH POMODORO SAUCE

This authentic Italian sauce has been in my family for years. I have used it on everything from baked potatoes to pasta. I have even used it as a tomato sauce for pizza.

1 pound linguine

1 28 ounce can chopped tomatoes

2 large shallots, chopped

3 cloves garlic, pressed

1 teaspoon sugar

¾ cup parmesan cheese, plus ½ cup for topping

2 tablespoons olive oil

Salt and ground pepper

1. In a large pan, sauté shallots in olive oil. When the shallots become soft, add garlic and cook for 1 minute.

2. Add the undrained can of chopped tomatoes to the onions and garlic and cook for 5 minutes.

3. Add sugar, season with salt and pepper and cook over medium heat for 20 minutes.

4. Remove sauce from heat, add parmesan cheese and mix thoroughly.

5. Process the tomato mixture in a food processor ¾ cup at a time until all sauce has been processed.

6. Boil 6 quarts of water and a drop of olive oil. Add linguine and cook for 10 to 11 minutes. Drain and place in a large bowl.

7. Pour pomodoro sauce over linguine and mix well. Serve with additional parmesan cheese. Serves 4.

PASTA IN PINK SAUCE WITH SUN DRIED TOMATOES & ARTICHOKES

✳ ✳ ✳

This fragrant pasta dish is a fabulous vegetarian option, which I often serve with my *Garden Vegetable Salad* and *Bruschetta*. Adding a cup of grilled chicken or shrimp also works well, if you are looking to add a bit more substance.

1 pound rotini pasta

2 cups Tomato Sauce (pg. 65)

1 cup cream

2 cloves garlic, pressed

½ cup parmesan cheese

1 14 ounce can artichoke hearts, quartered

6 to 8 sun dried tomatoes

1. Boil sun dried tomatoes in a small pan for 1to 2 minutes or until soft. Drain and cut into small pieces. Set aside.

2. Drain artichokes, trim away tough leaves and cut into small pieces. Set aside.

3. Add cream to the tomato sauce and stir until it becomes pink.

4. Boil 6 quarts of water and a drop of olive oil. Cook the pasta for 12 minutes, stirring occasionally.

5. Drain and add garlic, parmesan cheese, sun dried tomatoes and artichoke hearts.

6. Fold in pink sauce and serve. Serves 6.

CHICKEN PICCATA TENDERS

The tart capers really add to this dish, offering a refreshing change from traditional chicken tenders recipes. Any leftovers are great for a picnic lunch.

1 pound chicken tenders

Flour for dredging

½ cup milk

Salt and pepper

Juice of 1 lemon

2 tablespoons dry white wine

1½ tablespoons capers

4 tablespoons butter

2 tablespoons olive oil

4 tablespoons butter

1 tablespoon parsley, minced

1. Pour milk into a medium size bowl.

2. On a plate, combine flour, freshly ground pepper and salt and set aside.

3. Heat the oil and 4 tablespoons of butter in a large skillet. Dip tenders in milk, dredge in flour and place in skillet. Cook for 2 to 3 minutes on each side and transfer to a plate. Discard all but 2 tablespoons of the oil from the skillet.

4. Over low heat, add 4 tablespoons of butter, lemon and 2 tablespoons of wine. Cook for 2 minutes, stirring constantly.

5. Remove from heat. Add capers and parsley and pour over tenders. Serve immediately.

ANGEL HAIR PASTA WITH TOMATO, GARLIC & BROCCOLI

✳ ✳ ✳ ✳

This light and flavorful pasta dish is not only simple to prepare, but it is also high in nutrients. Highlighting superfoods such as tomatoes, garlic, broccoli and turkey, this is an especially healthy dish to throw together when your busy day just doesn't allow you to create a complex meal.

1 large tomato, diced

3 garlic cloves, minced

2 cups broccoli florets

½ cup basil flavored olive oil

½ cup extra virgin olive oil

1 cup parmesan cheese, grated

9 ounces angel hair pasta

Salt and pepper to taste

1 cup diced turkey (optional)

1. Steam broccoli for 2 to 3 minutes.

2. Combine all ingredients, except pasta, in large bowl. If you prefer, you can also add 1 cup of diced smoked turkey meat for extra protein and flavor. Set aside.

3. Boil 4 quarts of water in a large pot. Add pasta and cook for 2 minutes or until the pasta is al dente. Drain pasta and place in a large bowl.

4. Add vegetable mixture and stir until ingredients are well blended. Serve with additional parmesan cheese.

Note: If you are unable to find basil infused olive oil, substitute 1 cup of extra virgin olive oil mixed with 1 tablespoon of fresh chopped basil.

TURKEY BURGERS

✳ ✳ ✳ ✳

When compared with the traditional beef burger, turkey burgers tend to lack flavor. The shallots and red pepper in this version of the turkey burger really make it stand out as a family favorite. They are also healthy and low in fat!

1 pound ground turkey

½ cup of oats

½ cup mushrooms, diced

2 tablespoons olive oil

⅓ cup of red bell pepper, diced

1 large shallot, minced

1 large clove garlic, pressed

Salt and pepper

1. Place oats in a food processor and grind until almost a powder.

2. Sauté red pepper and shallots for 3 minutes in a small pan with 1 tablespoon of olive oil.

3. Add the mushrooms and garlic and sauté until fully cooked.

4. Place ground turkey in a large bowl. Add ground oats and mix completely with the turkey.

5. Add the mushroom and red pepper mixture and blend well.

6. With hands, form 4 turkey burger patties. Season with salt and pepper.

7. Add 1 tablespoon of olive oil to a medium size pan and cook turkey burgers for 4 minutes over medium heat. Flip and cook for an additional 4 to 5 minutes. The burger is fully cooked when you are able to press down on it with a spatula and no juice leaves the burger.

8. Serve with your choice of condiments. I like mayonnaise, ketchup, dill pickle slices and baby leaf spinach. I also like to serve it with Terra Sweet Potato Chips.

TURKEY CHILI

★ ★ ★ ★ ★ ★

My *Turkey Chili* goes well served with my *Garden Vegetable Salad* and corn muffins. If you prefer a spicier chili, simply increase the amount of cayenne.

2 pounds ground turkey

1 can chili beans

1 can kidney beans

1 onion, chopped

1 large clove garlic, minced

1 small can tomato paste

1 large can diced tomatoes

½ red bell pepper, diced

½ green bell pepper, diced

1 yellow chile pepper, diced

1 cup mushrooms, sliced

2 tablespoons chili powder

Dash of cayenne

¾ teaspoon cinnamon

1 tablespoon cider vinegar

2 tablespoons maple syrup

⅓ cup organic ketchup

Salt and pepper to taste

3 tablespoons olive oil

Grated cheddar cheese for topping (optional)

½ cup water if needed

1. In a large pot, sauté onion in olive oil until soft. Add yellow chili pepper, red and green bell peppers and cook for 1 minute.

2. Add garlic and turkey and cook over medium heat until turkey is done. Drain excess fat and return to stove.

3. Add mushrooms, chili powder, cinnamon, cayenne, salt, pepper, tomato paste, diced tomatoes, kidney beans, chili beans, cider vinegar, maple syrup and organic ketchup. Cook over low heat for 20 minutes. If chili seems a little dry, add water.

4. Serve topped with shredded cheddar cheese.

GARLIC CHICKEN STIR FRY

✳ ✳ ✳ ✳ ✳

This is a tasty dish that cooks very quickly, so it is important to have all ingredients measured out in separate bowls before you begin. This is a very healthy treat, containing five superfoods!

1 pound chicken breast tenders

¼ cup light olive oil, plus two tablespoons

2 cups broccoli

1 cup yellow baby corn (optional)

¾ cup cashews

1 medium onion

1 cup red bell pepper

1 tablespoon fresh ginger, minced

½ cup sliced water chestnuts

2 tablespoons rice wine vinegar

4 large cloves garlic, pressed

3 tablespoons soy sauce

¾ cup chicken broth

1 tablespoon cornstarch

1. Lightly season chicken with black pepper and cut into small strips.

2. Marinate chicken in ¼ cup olive oil, garlic and ginger for 45 minutes.

3. Cut onion and red pepper into thin, two inch strips.

4. Mix together chicken stock, soy sauce, rice wine vinegar and corn starch. Set aside.

5. In a large skillet, heat 2 tablespoons of light olive oil. Add chicken with marinade and stir fry for 2 minutes.

6. Add onions and peppers and cook for another 2 minutes.

7. Add broccoli, water chestnuts, corn and cashews. Cook an additional 2 minutes, making sure not to overcook the broccoli.

8. Stir in chicken stock mixture and bring to a boil while continuing to stir. This will take only 1 to 2 minutes.

9. Serve over brown rice.

TUNA STEAK IN PARCHMENT PAPER

The parchment paper keeps the tuna in this dish very moist. I prefer my tuna fully cooked and have prepared this recipe to my taste. However, if you prefer your tuna less cooked, simply reduce the cooking time to suit your palate.

4 tuna steaks

2 large shallots, diced

1 yellow bell pepper, diced

1 jalapeno pepper, minced

1 teaspoon cilantro, minced (optional)

1 lemon

2 tablespoons butter

2 tablespoons olive oil

Salt and pepper

4 pieces of parchment paper

Pats of butter

1. Preheat oven to 450 degrees.

2. Sauté shallots, jalapeno pepper and yellow pepper in 2 tablespoons of olive oil and 2 tablespoons of butter. When cooked, remove from heat and set aside.

3. Place each tuna steak on a piece of parchment paper, sprinkle with lemon juice, salt and pepper.

4. Top each tuna steak with a pat of butter and cover with sauté mixture.

5. Completely close parchment paper by twisting the ends. Bake for 10 to 12 minutes depending on the thickness of the tuna steaks.

6. Sprinkle with freshly chopped cilantro before serving.

Variation: Season with salt, pepper and lemon. Grill tuna for 5 minutes. Turn and add saute mixture on top. Grill for an additional 5 minutes. Remove from grill and sprinkle cilantro on top.

SPAGHETTI WITH GROUND TURKEY SAUCE

✹ ✹ ✹ ✹

My husband, Steve, refers to this dish as a gourmet version of the cafeteria spaghetti that grandmothers used to cook in schools many years ago. We like it a lot and have found that it is popular with kids of all ages.

1 small onion, diced

1 8 ounce container sliced mushrooms

½ cup red bell pepper, diced

¼ cup green bell pepper, diced

2 cloves garlic, minced

1 small can tomato paste

1 teaspoon sugar

1 28 ounce can diced tomatoes

½ cup black olives

2 teaspoons capers, rinsed

¼ cup parmesan cheese, shredded

1 pound ground turkey

Salt and pepper

1 teaspoon oregano

2 tablespoons olive oil

1 pound of spaghetti

1. Sauté onion, red pepper and green pepper in a large pan until onion is soft. Add garlic and sauté for 1 additional minute.

2. Add ground turkey, season with salt and pepper and fully cook.

3. Add tomato paste, tomatoes, sugar, and oregano. After cooking for 5 minutes add mushrooms.

4. When mushrooms are cooked, add black olives, capers and parmesan cheese.

5. In a large pot, boil 6 quarts of water and a drop of olive oil. Add spaghetti and cook for 9 to 11 minutes, stirring occasionally.

6. Drain spaghetti and add to turkey mixture. Serve with fresh parmesan cheese.

BOWTIE PASTA WITH PESTO

✳ ✳ ✳

There is nothing like cooking with fresh basil during the summer. It is such a fragrant herb and nothing showcases the versatility of its delicate flavor like this garden-fresh *Bowtie Pasta with Pesto.*

2 cups fresh basil leaves

½ cup parmesan cheese, grated

2 large cloves of garlic, pressed

4 tablespoons pine nuts

½ cup olive oil

Salt to taste

1 pound bowtie pasta

8 sun dried tomatoes

1 cup feta cheese, crumbled

1. Place pine nuts in a food processor and process until completely ground.

2. Add basil, parmesan cheese, garlic and salt. Lastly, add olive oil. Process until a smooth paste forms. Set aside.

3. Boil sun dried tomatoes for 2 minutes or until soft. Drain and cut into small pieces.

4. Boil 6 quarts of water with a dash of salt. Add pasta and cook for 12 minutes, stirring occasionally.

5. Drain pasta and pour into a large bowl. Add pesto and mix until pasta is well coated.

6. Add sun dried tomatoes and crumbled feta cheese and mix until evenly distributed throughout the pasta. Serve hot.

SALMON QUICHE WITH RICE CRUST

This delectable dish is a little more time consuming than most of my other dishes, but worth every minute. It makes a great brunch treat, served with fresh fruit, home made rolls and my *Blueberry Cake with Lemon Glaze* for dessert.

Crust:

1 cup brown rice

2 ¼ cups water

1 tablespoon butter

½ cup jack cheese

Dash of salt

⅓ cup onion, minced

½ cup cream cheese

1 egg, beaten

1. Bring water, butter, salt and uncooked rice to a boil in a pan. Stir once, cover and simmer for 45 minutes.

2. While the rice is cooking, lightly sprinkle the salmon with lemon and pepper. Wrap salmon in parchment paper and twist the ends to seal shut.

3. Place salmon in a pan of boiling water and poach for 10 minutes. Remove from heat and set aside.

4. Sauté peppers in 1 tablespoon of butter and set aside.

5. Sauté onion in 1 tablespoon of butter.

6. When rice is cooked, add onion to rice mixture and stir. Add ½ cup cream cheese and ½ cup of jack cheese and combine evenly. Once combined, add 1 beaten egg.

7. Press rice mixture into and up the sides of a buttered 9 x 9 x 2 inch baking dish.

8. Crumble the salmon into pieces and place on top of rice. Scatter the dill, peppers and corn randomly throughout the dish.

9. Mix together the eggs, half and half, and salt and pepper to taste.

Quiche:

½ pound poached salmon

4 eggs, beaten

*1 tablespoon fresh dill or
¼ teaspoon dill weed*

½ cup orange bell pepper

½ cup red bell pepper

½ cup frozen corn kernels

1 cup half and half

½ cup cream cheese

1 cup jack cheese

2 tablespoons butter

lemon

pepper

10. Pour egg mixture over dish and sprinkle 1 cup of jack cheese on top.

11. Place ½ cup of cream cheese cut into bite size pieces throughout the dish.

12. Bake at 350 degrees for 45 minutes.

GRILLED CHICKEN WITH CHARLES' MARINADE

I often prepare *Grilled Chicken with Charles' Marinade* when we entertain friends with small children, as it is a tasty treat that both kids and adults enjoy. It is especially good during the summer, served with potato salad, baked beans and corn on the cob. I also cut any leftovers I might have into strips and use them in my grilled chicken salad.

8 to 10 boneless chicken breasts

1 cup Worcestershire Sauce

4 tablespoons Colgin's Liquid Smoke

4 tablespoons Lawry's Lemon Pepper Seasoning

2 sticks butter

1 large onion, sliced

Juice of 1 lemon

Coarse ground pepper

1. Heat Worcestershire Sauce, liquid smoke, lemon pepper and butter in a medium size pan.

2. When butter is melted, add onion slices, lemon juice and ground pepper. Bring to a boil, then reduce heat, simmer and cook for 15 minutes.

3. Wash chicken breasts and put in container large enough for chicken and marinade. Pour marinade over chicken, along with onions and marinade for 30 minutes to an hour.

4. Grill chicken over an open flame for 4 to 5 minutes per side (depending on thickness of breast), while continually basting with marinade.

5. Put onions in foil or wire basket and cook on grill along with chicken. Top with onions before serving.

SALMON WITH GARLIC, TOMATOES & OLIVES

✴ ✴ ✴ ✴

This tasty, Mediterranean salmon dish contains no salt. There is just no need for it, as the sharp flavor of the olives and the natural acidity of the tomatoes, more than make up for it.

4 8 ounce salmon fillets

2 cloves garlic

Juice of 1 large lemon

6 tablespoons butter

1 carton cherry tomatoes

½ cup Kalamata olives, pitted

½ teaspoon dry thyme

Freshly ground pepper

1. Preheat oven to 425 degrees.

2. Put garlic through a press. Once pressed, add to food processor with lemon juice and butter. Process until blended.

3. Add the tomatoes and process until they are coarsely chopped.

4. Add Kalamata olives and thyme and process, on and off, until the mixture is chopped.

5. Place salmon in a lightly greased baking dish and season with freshly ground pepper. Spread the tomato and olive mixture on top of each filet.

6. Bake for 15 minutes or until salmon is fully cooked. Serve with freshly grated parmesan cheese.

SALMON BURGERS WITH BASIL SPREAD

✵ ✵ ✵ ✵

My *Salmon Burgers* are a great way to consume this amazing superfood. The *Pesto* and *Basil Spread* are very flavorful and complement the salmon incredibly well.

1 ¼ pound organic salmon

3 tablespoons olive oil

2 large shallots, minced

1 large lemon

4 tablespoons Pesto (pg. 90)

1 large egg, beaten

1 ½ cups plain bread crumbs

4 tablespoons marscapone cheese

Salt and ground pepper

Basil Spread (pg. 22)

6 whole wheat hamburger buns

Tomato slices

Lettuce

1. Over low heat, sauté shallots in 1 tablespoon of olive oil. When they begin to turn a golden color, remove from heat and set aside.
2. Remove skin from salmon (or ask butcher to trim for you). Rinse and cut into 3 inch pieces.
3. Squeeze lemon juice over salmon on both sides and process in food processor until it is completely ground.
4. Place salmon in large bowl, add shallot mixture and stir.
5. Add pesto, egg and mascarpone cheese and thoroughly blend.
6. Add bread crumbs and mix well.
7. Once blended, form 6 patties.
8. Line a platter with aluminum foil, place patties on platter and season both sides with salt and freshly ground pepper. Cover and refrigerate for 45 minutes to an hour.
9. In a large pan heat 2 tablespoons of olive oil. Place salmon patties in pan and cook for 2 to 3 minutes on each side.
10. Serve on bun with *Basil Spread*, lettuce and tomato.

SIDE DISHES

When I first began working on this cookbook, many of my friends asked me to include suggestions for side dishes that would compliment the entrees. With that in mind, I offer you several healthy options in the following section. Adding any of them to your meal will boost your intake of superfoods.

Although the following side dishes can be served with any of the entrees, some of them definitely work better with fish, while others work better with poultry or pasta. With fish, for example, I generally serve the *Wild Rice Salad, Garlic Snap Peas, Broccoli in Lemon Butter,* or *the Poppy Seed Coleslaw*. With chicken and turkey, the *Green Beans with Cashews, Curried Sweet Potato Salad* or any of the spinach dishes work really well. The *Buffalo Mozzarella with Tomatoes & Olives* enhances any of the pasta dishes, as does the *Red, Orange & Yellow Peppers with Olives*. The *Broccoli Pasta Salad* always makes a great accompaniment to the *Turkey Burgers and Salmon Burgers,* and the *Cucumber Raita* goes perfectly with the *Chicken Curry*. Ultimately, these are simply a few ideas to get you started. As always, it is a matter of taste. By taking time to experiment with different food combinations, I'm sure you'll discover what works best for you.

The superfoods featured in this section are: sweet potatoes, red, orange and yellow peppers, garlic, green beans, snap peas, cashews, broccoli, tomatoes, carrots, spinach, and cabbage.

Curried Sweet Potato Salad

Wild Rice Salad

Green Beans with Cashews

Cucumber Raita

Garlic Snap Peas

Buffalo Mozzarella with Tomatoes & Olives

Roasted Carrots in Balsamic Vinegar

Broccoli in Lemon Butter

Poppy Seed Coleslaw

Broccoli Pasta Salad

Spinach with Mushrooms

Spinach with Garlic & Parmesan Cheese

Red, Orange & Yellow Peppers with Olives

CURRIED SWEET POTATO SALAD

✳ ✳ ✳

Fear not! This side dish is actually quite mild, as it calls for a mild curry paste. It is sure to enhance your entrée, rather than overpower it.

3 large sweet potatoes

⅓ cup red bell pepper

⅓ cup green bell pepper

1 large shallot, diced

¼ cup roasted almond slices

1½ cups of mayonnaise

1 heaping tablespoon mild curry paste

2 heaping tablespoons honey

1 tablespoon olive oil

Salt and pepper to taste

Additional roasted almond slices for garnish

1. Peel potatoes and cut into ½ inch slices. Cut slices into pieces and place in a medium size pan with water. Boil for 7 minutes or until tender.

2. In a small bowl, combine mayonnaise, curry paste and honey. Set aside.

3. In a small pan, sauté shallots, red peppers and green peppers. Set aside.

4. When potatoes are done, drain in colander, place in a large bowl and sprinkle with almonds.

5. Add pepper mixture, salt and pepper. Pour curry sauce over potatoes and gently combine.

6. Transfer to serving dish and garnish edges with roasted almonds. Serves 6.

WILD RICE SALAD

✳ ✳ ✳ ✳

This makes a great side dish for the *Salmon Burgers, Turkey Burgers* or any of the fish entrees.

1 cup wild rice or wild rice blend

¼ cup pine nuts, toasted

2 tablespoons chives, finely minced

¼ cup red bell pepper, diced

¼ cup yellow bell pepper, diced

¼ cup orange bell pepper, diced

½ cup vinaigrette (pg. 61)

1 tablespoon fresh basil, cut into small strips

Salt and ground pepper to taste

1. Preheat oven to 250 degrees and toast pine nuts on baking sheet for 15 minutes or until slightly golden.

2. Rinse rice and place in a medium size pan with 2 cups of water and 2 teaspoons of olive oil. When rice starts to boil, cover pan with a tight lid and simmer for 40 to 45 minutes.

3. When rice is fully cooked, remove from heat and let cool for 5 minutes.

4. Place rice in a large bowl. Gently fold in pine nuts and chives.

5. Add peppers and gently stir.

6. Stir basil into the *Vinaigrette*, pour over the rice mixture and stir until blended. Add salt and pepper to taste. Add additional *Vinaigrette* to suit your taste.

Note: If you prefer, you can substitute my *Balsamic Vinaigrette* for the *Vinaigrette with Basil*.

GREEN BEANS WITH CASHEWS

This side dish is simple, easy and will compliment most any meal. I prefer to use oregano in this dish, but you may enjoy the flavor of another herb.

1 pound green beans, ends trimmed

1 large shallot, chopped

2 tablespoons light olive oil

1 cup roasted cashews, unsalted

¼ teaspoon oregano, dried

Salt and pepper to taste

1. Steam green beans for 4 to 5 minutes. Immerse in cold water to discontinue the cooking process and drain on paper towel.

2. Heat oil in large skillet. Add shallot and stir until shallot is soft.

3. Add green beans and cook for 2 to 3 minutes.

4. Add oregano, salt, pepper and cashews. Cook for an additional 30 seconds.

5. Remove from heat and transfer to serving dish.

CUCUMBER RAITA

I always serve this dish with the chicken curry. The cool cucumber perfectly compliments the spicy curry. When I serve it with a fish entrée, I omit the cumin and add ½ teaspoon of dill.

1 cucumber, peeled and sliced into quarters

1 tomato, chopped

1 cup plain yogurt

½ teaspoon cumin

Salt and white pepper

1. Combine cucumber and tomatoes in small bowl.
2. Add yogurt and stir.
3. Season with cumin, salt and pepper.
4. Stir again and transfer to serving bowl.

GARLIC SNAP PEAS

I love fresh snap peas and harvest them in my garden. Often, I simply steam them for 1 minute and eat them without a sauce, but garlic is always a tasty way to pep up any dish.

3 cups snap peas, ends trimmed

2 cloves garlic, minced

2 tablespoons olive oil

Salt and freshly ground pepper

1. In a large sauté pan, heat olive oil, add garlic and cook for approximately 30 seconds while continuously stirring.

2. Add the snap peas and stir for 2 minutes or until peas are cooked.

3. Remove from heat, season with salt and pepper and serve.

BUFFALO MOZZARELLA WITH TOMATOES & OLIVES

Anchoring the concept of the Mediterranean Diet, authentic Italian fare has always had a reputation for being fresh, healthy and largely uncomplicated. This delightful summer salad, featuring some of the vitamin and flavor packed foods typically consumed in the south of Italy, is a great example of how the simplest ingredients can be combined to create a single delectable dish. Thanks to my niece, Gretchen, who picked this recipe up while living in Italy.

2½ cups fresh mozzarella

1 container grape tomatoes

1 cup Kalamata olives

1 tablespoon dried oregano

⅓ cup extra virgin olive oil

1 tablespoon balsamic vinegar

Sea salt to taste

1. Cut mozzarella into 1 inch cubes and the grape tomatoes in half.

2. Combine first four ingredients in a mixing bowl and toss gently with extra virgin olive oil and balsamic vinegar.

3. Season with salt and transfer to a serving bowl.

4. Serve with fresh country Italian bread.

ROASTED CARROTS IN BALSAMIC VINEGAR

For this dish, I prefer to use a sweet balsamic vinegar, as opposed to one that is tart. It is the perfect match for the roasted carrots.

1 16 ounce bag baby carrots

1 tablespoon olive oil

Salt and ground pepper to taste

2 tablespoons balsamic vinegar

1 tablespoons chives, finely minced

1. Preheat oven to 450 degrees (or 425 degrees for a convection oven).

2. Wash carrots and place in large bowl.

3. Pour olive oil over carrots, add pepper and stir. Transfer to baking pan and cook for 15 minutes.

4. Remove carrots from oven and drizzle with balsamic vinegar. Cook for 3 additional minutes.

5. Remove carrots from oven and transfer to a large bowl. Add salt and chives. Stir, transfer to serving dish and serve.

Note: If you prefer, rosemary can be substituted for the chives.

BROCCOLI IN LEMON BUTTER

To cook or not to cook? That seems to be the undying question regarding the preparation of broccoli. My favorite method of preparing this super vegetable is to steam it for exactly three minutes, until it takes on a vivid green hue. At that point, the broccoli is no longer crunchy, but more importantly, it is not overcooked. Overcooking broccoli not only drains this incredibly healthy vegetable of many of its vital nutrients, but its texture becomes mushy as well. I particularly enjoy this dish, as the lemon butter adds a fresh zest.

2 cups broccoli florets, 1 inch stems

3 tablespoons butter

1 teaspoon lemon juice

Salt and pepper to taste

1 tablespoon toasted pine nuts (optional)

1. Melt butter in microwave in a medium size bowl.

2. Add lemon juice, salt and pepper (I find that just a dash of salt works best).

3. Add water to the bottom of a vegetable steamer. When water boils, add broccoli and cover. Cook for 3 minutes.

4. Remove broccoli from steamer and place in a bowl with the lemon butter. Fold broccoli into lemon butter and transfer to a serving dish.

Note: If desired, sprinkle 1 tablespoon of pine nuts over the dish before serving.

POPPY SEED COLESLAW

When I first experimented with this recipe, I used grated onion, which seemed to overpower the dish. Instead, the horseradish works perfectly.

6 cups cabbage, grated

¼ orange bell pepper, sliced

1 tablespoon chives, minced

2 tablespoons sour cream

¼ cup mayonnaise

2 tablespoons horseradish

2 tablespoons pineapple juice

¾ teaspoon poppy seeds

¼ cup raisins

1. Place grated cabbage in large bowl. Add chives and orange bell pepper.

2. Add remaining ingredients and stir thoroughly.

3. Transfer to serving dish.

Note: If you prefer, you can substitute celery seeds for the poppy seeds.

BROCCOLI PASTA SALAD

✖ ✖ ✖ ✖

Pasta salads are always a great way to incorporate all of your favorite vegetables into your diet. My version combines a combination of superfoods that harmoniously blend together to form an easy, healthy and positively delectable treat that can be served on its own or as a tasty side dish. I also enjoy using the red and orange pepper sauce as a spread, particularly on a smoked turkey sandwich with tomatoes and baby Swiss cheese.

8 ounces small shell pasta

2½ cups broccoli florets

8 ounces hearts of palm, tips and cuts

¾ cup Kalamata olives, halved

1 red bell pepper, roasted

1 orange bell pepper, roasted

1 large clove garlic, pressed

1¾ cups mayonnaise

1. In a medium sized pan, bring 4 quarts of water to a boil. Add pasta and cook for 12 minutes, stirring occasionally.

2. While pasta is cooking, steam the broccoli florets for 2 to 3 minutes.

3. Remove the broccoli from the steamer and immerse in cold water. This technique serves to halt the cooking process, as it is important not to overcook the broccoli.

4. Remove broccoli from cold water and place on paper towel to drain.

5. Place roasted peppers in food processor and process until smooth.

6. Add garlic and mayonnaise. Process until well combined.

7. When pasta is prepared, drain and place in a large bowl. Add hearts of palm, Kalamata olives and broccoli.

8. Fold red and orange pepper mixture into pasta until combined. Transfer to a serving dish.

SPINACH WITH MUSHROOMS

✹ ✹

This flavorful side dish goes well with the Chicken Piccata Tenders.

2 16 ounce bags spinach

3 large shallots, diced

1 8 ounce container mushrooms, sliced

½ cup of Alouette cheese with garlic and herbs

1 tablespoon fresh rosemary (or 1 teaspoon dried rosemary)

2 tablespoons olive oil

Salt and pepper

1. In a small bowl, combine rosemary and alouette cheese and set aside.

2. In a large pan, sauté shallots in olive oil until soft. Add mushrooms.

3. Once mushrooms soften, add spinach, salt and pepper to taste. Continue cook for 2 minutes or until spinach reduces.

4. Remove from heat and drain.

5. Fold in cheese mixture, transfer to serving dish and serve.

SPINACH WITH GARLIC & PARMESAN CHEESE

This side dish is very flavorful and so simple to prepare. Because spinach shrinks when cooked, be sure that you have enough for the amount of people you are serving.

2 10 ounce bags baby spinach

2 cloves garlic, pressed

1 tablespoon extra virgin olive oil

¼ cup freshly grated parmesan cheese

Salt and pepper

1. In large sauté pan, heat olive oil.

2. Add spinach, garlic, salt and pepper. Cover pan and cook for 2 minutes or until the spinach has wilted.

3. Remove from heat and drain excess liquid.

4. Sprinkle with parmesan cheese and transfer to serving dish.

RED, ORANGE & YELLOW PEPPERS WITH OLIVES

✳ ✳ ✳ ✳

This is simple, light and delicious side is another healthy dish my niece, Gretchen, picked up while living in Italy. It perfectly accompanies fish, chicken or turkey.

2 red peppers

2 orange peppers

2 yellow peppers

2 tomatoes, chopped or 1 carton of grape tomatoes

½ cup of fresh green olives, pitted

2 tablespoons capers

1 to 2 cloves garlic, pressed

Italian parsley (can substitute basil if desired)

Extra virgin olive oil

Sea salt to taste

1. Roast peppers under broiler in oven or on grill.

2. Peel, rinse, devein and deseed peppers.

3. Cut peppers into strips and place in mixing bowl. Add tomatoes, olives, capers, garlic and Italian parsley.

4. Season with sea salt and toss with extra virgin olive oil.

5. Transfer to serving bowl and serve at room temperature with dense Italian country bread.

BREAKFAST

Breakfast is the most vital meal that we consume. While it is important to fuel our bodies with enough food to sustain us and give us energy, it is not simply a question of quantity. Instead, both the quantity and the quality of food we consume as we start our day impacts our overall health and wellbeing. For this reason, it is important to incorporate the superfoods into our morning meal.

During the week, I usually alternate between having a bowl of oatmeal and eating a sprouted wheat bagel with sliced tomatoes or organic reduced fat cream cheese for breakfast. I usually have an early destination, so I try to eat quickly, but healthy. Most of the recipes I include in this book are dishes that I prepare for my family on the weekends, when we all have a bit more time to relax and enjoy ourselves.

The great thing about the breakfast treats that you will find on the pages that follow is that many of them also make great gifts, particularly the *Nutty Granola*, the *Blueberry Pecan Muffins* and the *Oat Scones*. Also, the *Nutty Granola* makes a delicious snack for when you are on the run and just need a little something healthy to energize you and tide you over until your next meal.

The superfoods featured in this section include: oats, blueberries, pumpkin, broccoli, spinach, red pepper, turkey, salmon, pecans, walnuts and almonds.

Nutty Granola

Blueberry Pecan Muffins

Vegetable Frittata

Scrambled Eggs with Tomatoes & Cream Cheese

Blueberry Waffles

Scones with Oats & Dried Blueberries

Pumpkin Waffles with Pecan Maple Syrup

Oatmeal

Spinach Omelet with White Cheddar Cheese

Quiche with Turkey Bacon, Tomatoes & Avocado

Salmon, Eggs & Shallots

NUTTY GRANOLA

✳ ✳ ✳ ✳

Once you make home made granola, you will never go back to the packaged granola. For breakfast, I usually serve it with fresh blueberries and milk. However, when I am in a hurry and need a quick snack, I grab a handful and go!

4 cups rolled oats

2 cups sliced almonds

1 cup walnut pieces

½ cup dried currants

1 cup pecan pieces

½ cup canola oil

½ cup honey

½ cup maple syrup

1 teaspoon cinnamon

1. Preheat the oven to 350 degrees.

2. In large bowl, combine oats, almonds, walnuts and pecans. Set aside.

3. In small bowl stir together canola oil, honey, maple syrup and cinnamon. Pour over oats and nuts and coat evenly.

4. Pour granola mixture onto lightly greased cookie sheet and bake for 30 minutes or until the granola has an even brown color.

5. While the granola is baking, turn the granola over with a spatula every 10 minutes to ensure that it bakes evenly.

6. Remove granola from the oven and let it cool.

7. Return to bowl, add currants and mix.

8. Store in airtight container.

BLUEBERRY PECAN MUFFINS

I enjoy my *Blueberry Pecan Muffins* with a hot cup of green tea on lazy Sunday afternoons. In this recipe, I finely grind the pecans, which creates a luscious pecan flavored muffin dotted throughout with fresh, whole blueberries. This unique method allows you to enjoy the delectable taste of pecans with every bite!

2¼ cups cake flour

1 egg, beaten

¾ cups sugar

1 cup milk

1 stick butter

1 tablespoon baking powder

½ teaspoon salt

½ teaspoon vanilla

¾ cup blueberries

½ cup pecans

1. Preheat oven to 425 degrees (400 degrees if using a convection oven).

2. Combine all dry ingredients, except for the pecans, in a large mixing bowl.

3. Use food processor to finely grind the pecans and then add them to the dry ingredients.

4. Fold in blueberries and set aside.

5. Melt butter in microwave. In a small bowl, combine melted butter with milk, vanilla and eggs and fold into dry ingredients until completely mixed. Be careful not to over blend.

6. Butter a muffin tin or line tin with baking cups. Fill muffin tins ⅔ full. You can add a little more if you prefer a fuller muffin. Just don't fill to the top! Bake for 15 minutes. Makes 12 muffins.

VEGETABLE FRITTATA

For this dish, I use Leerdammer, a baby Swiss cheese from Holland. While common in Europe, it can sometimes be difficult to find in the US. I purchase it from my local health food store or specialty market. It has a delicious, rich and nutty flavor that is worth the extra effort!

6 eggs, beaten

3 tablespoons cream

½ cup broccoli florets

½ cup red pepper, diced

½ cup mushrooms, sliced

1 tablespoon chives

1 cup Leerdammer cheese, grated

4 tablespoons butter

2 tablespoons light olive oil

Salt and freshly ground pepper

1. Preheat oven to 450 degrees.

2. Sauté the mushrooms and red pepper in 1 tablespoon of butter and 1 tablespoon of olive oil.

3. After the red pepper softens, add broccoli and cook for 2 minutes. Set aside.

4. In a medium size bowl, combine eggs, cream, salt, pepper and chives.

5. Heat 2 tablespoons of butter and 1 tablespoon of olive oil in a large skillet. Pour egg mixture in pan and cook on low heat.

6. When mixture is still soft on top, remove from heat. Sprinkle mushrooms, red pepper, broccoli and cheese on top of eggs and drizzle with 1 tablespoon of butter.

7. Place pan in oven and bake until cheese has melted. Watch closely, as it will only take about 3 minutes to fully cook.

8. Remove and transfer to serving dish.

SCRAMBLED EGGS WITH TOMATOES & CREAM CHEESE

I don't prepare this dish very often, but when I do, it gets rave reviews. I like to serve it with warm raisin toast and fresh orange juice. It literally melts in your mouth!

6 eggs

1 tablespoon milk

1 tomato, chopped

1 small package cream cheese, cut into small pieces

2 tablespoons butter

Salt and pepper to taste

1. In a medium size bowl, beat eggs, milk, salt and pepper with a whisk or fork until the mixture is well combined.

2. In a large pan, add butter and heat on medium until melted. Pour eggs into pan and stir.

3. When eggs are almost fully scrambled, add tomatoes and cream cheese. Cook 1 additional minute.

4. Remove from heat and serve immediately.

BLUEBERRY WAFFLES

I love waking my husband up with the fragrant aroma of my fresh *Blueberry Waffles* on Sunday mornings. He loves the sweet, yet tart, flavor of the blueberries and I think they're simply scrumptious, especially when drenched in organic maple syrup and dusted with powdered sugar.

2 cups organic flour

2½ teaspoons baking powder

1 teaspoon salt

¼ cup sugar

2 eggs, separated

1½ cups milk

6 tablespoons canola oil

¾ cup fresh blueberries

1. Sift together flour, baking powder, salt and sugar. Set aside.

2. Add milk and canola oil to lightly beaten egg yolks. Stir in flour mixture until moistened, leaving the batter lumpy.

3. Add blueberries.

4. Beat egg whites until they form firm peaks, then fold into batter.

5. Grease heated waffle iron with cooking spray. Pour batter evenly into waffle iron and cook until lightly brown.

6. Serve with additional blueberries as a garnish.

SCONES WITH OATS & DRIED BLUEBERRIES

✹ ✹

I received my inspiration for this recipe from the book *Simply Scones*, by Leslie Weiner and Barbara Albright. In my version, I use organic flour and add ground oats, honey, and dried blueberries, to create a special superfood enhanced treat.

2 cups organic all-purpose flour

¼ cup sugar

2 tablespoons honey

2 teaspoons baking powder

⅛ teaspoon salt

½ cup ground oats

⅓ cup butter, chilled

½ cup heavy whipping cream

1 egg

1½ teaspoons vanilla

½ cup dried blueberries

1. Preheat oven to 425 degrees. Lightly grease a baking sheet.

2. In a large bowl, stir together all dry ingredients.

3. Cut butter into pieces and distribute it throughout the flour mixture. Mix until coarse crumbs form.

4. In a small bowl, stir together the cream, honey, egg and vanilla.

5. Add the cream mixture to the flour mixture and stir until blended.

6. Add the blueberries and stir.

7. With lightly floured hands and rolling pin, roll dough out on a board to about ½ inch thick. If the dough is too moist to handle, add additional flour to the board and to your hands as you work with the mixture.

8. Use a floured biscuit cutter or cookie cutter to cut out scones. Gather scraps and repeat until all dough is used.

9. Place on baking sheet and bake for 12 minutes or until lightly browned. Makes about 18 scones.

Note: Scones are typically served with clotted cream and hot tea in England. I serve these with an organic blueberry spread and either an Earl Grey or green tea.

PUMPKIN WAFFLES WITH PECAN MAPLE SYRUP

These hearty, spiced waffles make the perfect treat for a crisp fall morning when served with turkey bacon or turkey sausage.

2 cups all purpose flour

1 teaspoon salt

2½ teaspoon baking powder

2 large eggs, separated

4 tablespoon canola oil

1½ cups milk

¼ cup sugar

¾ cup pumpkin

1 teaspoon cinnamon

1 teaspoon vanilla

½ cup chopped pecans

1 cup maple syrup

1. In a small bowl, sift together flour, salt and baking powder. Add cinnamon and sugar. Combine and set aside.

2. In large bowl, combine egg yolks, canola oil, pumpkin, milk and vanilla.

3. Gradually add flour mixture to egg mixture.

4. Beat egg whites until they form firm peaks. Fold into batter.

5. Spray hot waffle iron with cooking spray and pour batter into the center of the iron. Cook waffle until golden brown.

6. Remove and transfer to serving plate.

7. Add pecans to maple syrup and heat in microwave for 20 seconds. Pour over waffle and serve immediately.

OATMEAL

✶ ✶ ✶

Oatmeal is so healthy, so I wanted to share a few ways that I keep it appetizing. Because instant oatmeal has less fiber and nutritional value, and it often contains sugar and other additives, I always prefer to use whole oats.

Blueberry, Walnuts &
Maple Syrup:

½ cup whole oats

1 cup water

¼ cup blueberries

¼ cup walnut pieces

2 tablespoons organic
maple syrup

Banana, Pecans & Honey:

½ banana, sliced

¼ cup pecan pieces

1 tablespoon honey

Dash of cinnamon

Currants & Almonds:

½ cup oats

1 cup milk

¼ cup currants or raisins

¼ cup sliced almonds

1. Place oats and water in bowl and cook in microwave for 2 minutes and 15 seconds. Remove from microwave. Add blueberries and stir. Add walnuts and maple syrup and stir. Serves 1.

2. Alternatively, you can substitute the blueberries, walnuts and maple syrup for banana, pecan pieces, honey and a dash of cinnamon.

3. If you prefer your oatmeal with currants and almonds, heat 1 cup of milk on the stove in a small pan. When the milk begins to boil, add oats. Stir and cook over medium heat for 5 minutes or until fully cooked. Remove from heat. Top with currants (or raisins) and almond slices. Serve immediately.

SPINACH OMELET WITH WHITE CHEDDAR CHEESE

I especially love this omelet because it is both easy to prepare and tasty. It is the perfect way to slip healthy spinach into the diet of a loved one who doesn't particularly care for it.

2 eggs, lightly beaten

1 teaspoon water

1 small shallot, diced

½ cup baby spinach, stems removed

¼ cup mushrooms, sliced

⅓ cup white cheddar cheese, shredded

4 teaspoons olive oil

2 tablespoons butter

Salt and pepper

1. In a small pan, heat 2 teaspoons of olive oil and 1 tablespoon of butter. Add shallots and mushrooms.

2. When shallots become soft, add spinach, cover and cook for 2 minutes. Remove the cover from the pan and set aside.

3. In a small bowl, beat eggs, water, salt and pepper until light and foamy.

4. In a medium pan, heat remaining olive oil and butter. When butter has melted, add eggs. Swirl pan to cook eggs. If there is a lot of liquid remaining, pull the sides of the omelet up from the edge to allow the liquid to run underneath.

5. When eggs are slightly moist on top, but set on bottom, place spinach mixture on half of omelet nearest you. Sprinkle cheese on spinach mixture.

6. Lift the pan off of the stove and hold it at an angle. Gently roll the omelet in half with a spatula. Wait 10 to 15 seconds before transferring to plate in order to allow the cheese to melt.

QUICHE WITH TURKEY BACON, TOMATOES & AVOCADO

This is a great dish to serve when you have guests, as it can be made ahead of time and reheated in the microwave. It goes wonderfully with hash browns and fruit.

6 *slices wheat bread, trimmed and cut into strips*

Butter for greasing dish

4 eggs

1½ cups jack cheese

1½ cups light cream

4 strips turkey bacon

1 tomato, chopped

1 tablespoon chives, minced

½ avocado, diced

Salt and pepper

1. Preheat oven to 375 degrees. Butter 9 inch round quiche pan.

2. Line pan with bread strips and press evenly into the sides and bottom of pan. Set aside.

3. In a separate pan, cook bacon, drain on a paper towel and crumble. Set aside.

4. In a small bowl, beat eggs, cream, salt and pepper. Set aside.

5. Sprinkle tomato and crumbled bacon on bread strips. Add chives, avocado and cheese.

6. Pour egg mixture over top of cheese and let stand for 20 minutes. Bake for 40 minutes or until golden brown.

Note: If you prefer, you can omit the turkey bacon, tomatoes and avocado and add 1 pound of cooked turkey sausage and ½ cup of sautéed red pepper.

SALMON, EGGS & SHALLOTS

This is my version of the classic *Lox, Eggs & Onions,* which my husband often requests.

6 eggs

1 tablespoon milk

1 tablespoon chives, finely minced

1 shallot, minced

3 ounces smoked salmon, cut into bite size pieces

¼ cup mascarpone cheese

1 tablespoon butter

1 tablespoon light olive oil
pepper

1. In a medium size bowl, whisk eggs, milk, salt and pepper.

2. In a large sauté pan, sauté shallots in butter and oil until soft.

3. Add egg mixture and cook until softly scrambled

4. Add mascarpone cheese. Once cheese is folded into eggs, add salmon and stir.

5. Transfer to serving dish, sprinkle with chives and serve.

DESSERTS

What cookbook would be complete without a section dedicated to desserts? Thankfully, even decadent desserts can contain superfoods. This section of the book is intended for special occasions not for every day indulgence.

When it comes to desserts, all of my close friends and family will tell you that I am a "Chocolaterian." I willingly confess that they are right. I take my chocolate seriously and admit to having a healthy obsession with the rich taste and aroma of this decadent dessert item. Fortunately, chocolate has been touted a superfood for the beneficial flavonoids contained in the cocoa. Thank you, God! It is, therefore, with much pleasure that I list a few heavenly desserts featuring chocolate as an honorable mention.

Just as in the other sections of this book, some of my desserts are lighter than others and work well when served to guests after a light lunch, such as the *Pumpkin Bread* and *Almond Cake*. Others, such as the *White & Milk Chocolate Blondie Bars* and the *Dark Chocolate Truffles Rolled in Pistachios,* are richer and make great treats to serve either after a meal or on their own with green tea. Whatever the occasion, I'm confident that you will find a special dessert to suit the taste of both you and your guests.

The superfoods featured in this section include: blueberries, oats, pumpkin, sweet potatoes, almonds, pistachios, walnuts, pecans and carrots.

BLUEBERRY CAKE WITH LEMON GLAZE

When I first experimented with this cake, I topped it with a glaze of brown sugar, cinnamon and walnuts. It was much more of a breakfast cake. This version is moist and flavorful and features a hint of lemon that makes a fabulous dessert. I am really happy with it and I hope you will be too!

2 ½ cups all purpose flour

1 cup sour cream

1 cup blueberries

1 ½ cups sugar, plus 3 tablespoons for blueberry mixture

2 teaspoons baking soda

1 cup butter

2 eggs

1 teaspoon vanilla

½ teaspoon salt

Juice of ½ lemon

Glaze:

¾ cup powdered sugar

2 tablespoons milk

1 tablespoon fresh lemon juice

1. Preheat oven to 350 degrees.

2. Grease and flour a 9 inch tube pan.

3. Combine flour, baking soda and salt in a small bowl and set aside.

4. In a separate bowl, add blueberries and 3 tablespoons of sugar.

5. In a large bowl with mixer, cream butter and add sugar, lemon juice and vanilla.

6. Add eggs, one at a time, as you continue to mix.

7. Add sour cream and slowly combine cream mixture with flour mixture until completely blended.

8. Fold blueberries into mixture. Pour evenly into 9 inch tube pan.

9. Bake at 350 degrees for 50 minutes. Remove from oven and let cool.

10. Once cooled, pour glaze over top. Garnish with fresh blueberries.

PUMPKIN BREAD

My family enjoys the spiced flavor of my *Pumpkin Bread* during the fall when the leaves begin to change color and the temperature drops. This is a moist, light treat that I often serve with hot tea when I have company.

3 cups organic all purpose flour

1 teaspoon baking soda

½ teaspoon salt

¾ teaspoon baking powder

2 teaspoons cinnamon

1 teaspoon ground cloves

1 teaspoon nutmeg

¼ teaspoon mace

2 cups canned pumpkin

2 cups sugar

3 eggs, beaten

½ teaspoon vanilla

1 cup canola oil

1. Preheat oven to 325 degrees. Grease and flour two 9 inch loaf pans.

2. In a medium size bowl, sift together the flour, salt, baking soda, baking powder, cinnamon, cloves, mace and nutmeg.

3. In a large bowl, blend sugar and oil with an electric mixer.

4. Add eggs and beat until well blended.

5. Add pumpkin and vanilla and continue to beat.

6. Gradually add flour mixture to pumpkin mixture.

7. Once blended, pour in pans and bake for 1 hour. Remove from oven and cool in pans.

CARROT CAKE

This cake is incredibly moist and very easy to make. It is so scrumptious, that my husband requests it every year on his birthday.

Cake:

2 cups organic all purpose flour

2 teaspoon baking soda

½ teaspoon salt

2 teaspoons cinnamon

4 eggs

3 cups grated carrots

2 cups sugar

1½ cups canola oil

½ cup walnuts

Cream Cheese Icing:

1 box confectioner's sugar

1 8 ounce package cream cheese

1 stick unsalted butter

1½ teaspoons vanilla

1. Preheat oven to 350 degrees. Grease and flour two 9 inch round pans.

2. In medium size bowl, sift together flour, baking soda, salt and cinnamon.

3. In large bowl, combine sugar and oil. Add flour mixture to oil mixture and blend. Gently fold carrots and walnuts into mixture.

4. Pour evenly into cake pans and bake for 30 minutes or until an inserted toothpick comes out clean. Allow to cool completely.

5. For the icing, cream together the butter and cheese in a small bowl. Once combined, add vanilla. Gradually add sugar until completely blended.

ALMOND CAKE

The holiday season is always such a special time for my family. Every year, several of us gather at my sister Pam's house to celebrate a season full of love, good spirit and great food. Although we cannot remember the origin of this recipe, Pam has made this cake throughout the years and was generous enough to share it with us.

1½ cups all purpose flour

⅛ teaspoon salt

¾ cup butter

2 eggs

1 teaspoon almond flavoring

¾ cup sliced almonds

1½ cups sugar

1. Preheat oven to 350 degrees.

2. Melt butter and combine with sugar.

3. Use a mixer to combine remaining ingredients.

4. Completely line a 9 inch skillet with heavy foil and grease with butter.

5. Fill skillet with batter and sprinkle with sliced almonds and sugar.

6. Bake for 30 to 40 minutes or until golden brown.

FUDGE BROWNIES WITH WALNUTS

These brownies are simple to make and will satisfy any chocolate lover. In some of my desserts, I have experimented with different types of nuts. However, with my *Fudge Brownies*, I have found that the classic combination of chocolate and walnuts works best.

1 cup flour

1 teaspoon baking powder

⅛ teaspoon salt

1 cup butter, melted

4 eggs

⅓ cup sour cream

4 unsweetened chocolate squares

2 cups sugar

2 teaspoons vanilla

½ cup chopped walnuts

1. Preheat oven to 350 degrees.

2. In a small bowl, combine flour, baking powder and salt. Set aside.

3. Melt chocolate in a double boiler.

4. In a large bowl, combine melted butter and sugar. Add sour cream, eggs, and vanilla. Add chocolate and stir until blended.

5. Add flour mixture to chocolate mixture and stir.

6. Add walnuts and stir.

7. Spread evenly in a 9 x 13 inch pan and bake for 20 minutes.

OATMEAL ALMOND COOKIES

I created these special cookies with my niece, Gretchen, in mind. She doesn't care for walnuts or pecans and I wanted to design a cookie that she would enjoy. Not only does she love them, but they have become my husband's favorite cookie too!

1½ cups all purpose flour

1 teaspoon baking soda

½ teaspoon salt

½ teaspoon cinnamon

1½ cups uncooked oats

1 cup butter

1 cup light brown sugar

½ cup white sugar

1 large egg

1 teaspoon vanilla

¾ cup sliced almonds

½ cup milk chocolate chips

1. Preheat oven to 375 degrees (350 degrees if using a convection oven).

2. In a medium size bowl, sift together flour, baking soda, salt and cinnamon.

3. Add oats and mix with a large spoon to distribute throughout the flour. Set aside.

4. In a medium size pan, cream together the butter, brown sugar and white sugar.

5. When sugar has dissolved, add egg and vanilla. Stir.

6. Gradually add flour mixture to butter mixture.

7. When combined, add almonds and chocolate chips.

8. Drop 2 tablespoons of dough per cookie onto lightly greased cookie sheet, leaving approximately 2 inches between cookies. I usually bake 6 cookies at a time so that they have enough room to spread out. If your oven can accommodate a larger cookie sheet, you can cook more than six at a time.

9. Bake for 12 minutes. Remove from oven and allow to cool for 2 minutes.

10. Remove cookies from cookie sheet with a spatula and place on a paper towel to cool thoroughly. Store in airtight container. Makes 2 dozen.

BLUEBERRY TART

A good friend of mine, who doesn't particularly care for blueberries, asked me to come up with a great blueberry dessert that she can enjoy with her husband, who absolutely loves them. The solution? My luscious, sweet *Blueberry Tart!* Now, even she is a devoted blueberry fan!

Crust:

1 cup flour

1 stick butter

⅓ cup walnuts, chopped

Blueberry Mixture:

4 cups fresh blueberries

Juice of ½ lemon

¾ cup sugar

Topping:

1 cup whipping cream

3 tablespoons of confectioner's sugar

1. Preheat oven to 350 degrees.

2. Blend flour and butter until it resembles coarse meal. Add chopped walnuts.

3. Form crust by pressing flour mixture into the bottom and half way up the side of a 9 inch round glass pan.

4. Bake for 15 minutes or until golden brown. Let crust cool completely before adding blueberry mixture.

5. In saucepan, add 2 cups of blueberries with the lemon and sugar. Cook over low heat until sugar dissolves.

6. Once sugar has dissolved, increase temperature and bring mixture to a boil. Boil for approximately 10 minutes, stirring continuously, until the mixture becomes thick.

7. Allow mixture to cool and add the remaining 2 cups of raw berries.

8. Pour the blueberry mixture into the crust.

9. Combine whipping cream and sugar in food processor. Blend until cream thickens and spread evenly over the top of the tart. Garnish with fresh blueberries. Refrigerate.

SWEET POTATO PIE

I serve my Sweet Potato Pie as an alternative to pumpkin pie at Thanksgiving. It is similar in flavor, but not too sweet. I especially love how the diverse textures of this dessert keep it interesting.

Pie Crust:

2¼ cups graham cracker crumbs

1 stick butter, melted

2 tablespoons sugar

2 tablespoons ground pecans

Filling:

1 large sweet potato, cooked

¾ cup sugar

2 tablespoons butter, melted

3 eggs, beaten

1 tablespoon lemon juice

1 tablespoon maple syrup

½ teaspoon cinnamon

½ teaspoon salt

¼ teaspoon nutmeg

¼ teaspoon mace

½ cup cream

Topping:

½ cup light brown sugar

4 tablespoons butter

½ cup flour

½ cup chopped pecans

1. Preheat oven to 375 degrees.

2. For the crust, combine ingredients and press into 9 inch deep pie pan. Chill for 15 minutes.

3. In a small bowl, blend together the light brown sugar, butter and flour until crumbs form. Add chopped pecans and mix well.

4. In a large bowl, beat sweet potatoes, maple syrup and sugar with an electric mixer.

5. While continuing to beat, add butter, spices, vanilla and lemon juice.

6. Gradually add the eggs and cream. Blend until smooth and pour into pie crust.

7. Bake for 30 minutes. Add pecan topping and cook for an additional 10 minutes.

WHITE & MILK CHOCOLATE BLONDIE BARS

This is a chocolate lover's playground! I must admit, I had to sacrifice my favorite jeans in order to create this recipe…but it was worth it!

6 tablespoons unsalted butter

1 egg

1 cup all purpose flour

1 teaspoon baking powder

dash of salt

1 cup light brown sugar

1 teaspoon vanilla

4 ounces white baking chocolate, chopped

½ cup milk chocolate chips

½ cup chopped pecans

1. Preheat oven to 350 degrees. Grease and flour a 9 x 9 inch square pan.

2. In small bowl, stir together flour, salt and baking powder. Set aside.

3. In a large bowl, use an electric mixer to cream together the butter that is softened and sugar.

4. When the butter mixture is smooth, add egg and vanilla. Mix until well blended.

5. Gradually add flour mixture to butter mixture and blend.

6. Use a spatula to fold white chocolate, chocolate chips and pecans into the mixture.

7. Spread batter evenly in pan and bake for 20 minutes. Allow to cool completely and cut into squares. Store in an air tight container.

DARK CHOCOLATE TRUFFLES ROLLED IN PISTACHIOS

These truffles are so delicious that you will not believe how easy they are to make! I use Callebaut chocolate, which is my favorite baking chocolate. However, Ghirardelli's baking chocolate also works very well.

12 ounces semisweet chocolate, grated

1 cup cream

1 teaspoon of hazelnut extract

2 cups pistachios, ground

Strawberries for garnish (optional)

1. Use the grater blade of your food processor to grate the chocolate. If you don't have a food processor, simply break the chocolate into small pieces with a knife.

2. Once grated, place chocolate in a large bowl and set aside.

3. In the food processor, grind pistachios and pour them onto a large plate. Set aside.

4. Heat cream in a small pan. When cream begins to boil, pour over chocolate and stir until it has completely melted and the chocolate is smooth. Stir hazelnut extract into chocolate.

5. Refrigerate for 1 to 2 hours, until the chocolate feels firm enough to roll.

6. Take 1 tablespoon of chocolate and roll into a ball. Roll the truffle in the pistachios and place in a paper candy cup or on a dessert plate. If serving the truffles on a plate, garnish with fresh strawberries.

Note: As an alternative to the pistachios, you can also roll the truffles in ground walnuts or powdered sugar.

INDEX

NOTES: